teach® yourself

film making

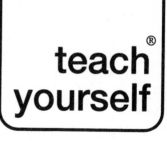

film making
tom holden

Launched in 1938, the **teach yourself** series
grew rapidly in response to the world's wartime
needs. Loved and trusted by over 50 million
readers, the series has continued to respond to
society's changing interests and passions and
now, 70 years on, includes over 500 titles,
from Arabic and Beekeeping to Yoga and Zulu.
What would you like to learn?

be where you want to be with **teach yourself**

For UK order enquiries: please contact Bookpoint Ltd, 130 Milton Park, Abingdon, Oxon, OX14 4SB. Telephone: +44 (0) 1235 827720. Fax: +44 (0) 1235 400454. Lines are open 09.00–17.00, Monday to Saturday, with a 24-hour message answering service. Details about our titles and how to order are available at www.teachyourself.co.uk

For USA order enquiries: please contact McGraw-Hill Customer Services, PO Box 545, Blacklick, OH 43004-0545, USA. Telephone: 1-800-722-4726. Fax: 1-614-755-5645.

For Canada order enquiries: please contact McGraw-Hill Ryerson Ltd, 300 Water St, Whitby, Ontario L1N 9B6, Canada. Telephone: 905 430 5000. Fax: 905 430 5020.

Long renowned as the authoritative source for self-guided learning – with more than 50 million copies sold worldwide – the **teach yourself** series includes over 500 titles in the fields of languages, crafts, hobbies, business, computing and education.

British Library Cataloguing in Publication Data: a catalogue record for this title is available from the British Library.

Library of Congress Catalog Card Number: on file.

First published in UK 2002 by Hodder Education, part of Hachette Live UK, 338 Euston Road, London, NW1 3BH.

First published in US 2002 by The McGraw-Hill Companies, Inc.

This edition published 2007.

The **teach yourself** name is a registered trade mark of Hodder Headline.

Copyright © 2002, 2003, 2007 Tom Holden

Typeset by Transet Limited, Coventry, England.
Printed in Great Britain for Hodder Education, an Hachette Livre UK Company, 338 Euston Road, London NW1 3BH, by Cox & Wyman Ltd, Reading, Berkshire.

The publisher has used its best endeavours to ensure that the URLs for external websites referred to in this book are correct and active at the time of going to press. However, the publisher and the author have no responsibility for the websites and can make no guarantee that a site will remain live or that the content will remain relevant, decent or appropriate.

Hachette Livre UK's policy is to use papers that are natural, renewable and recyclable products and made from wood grown in sustainable forests. The logging and manufacturing processes are expected to conform to the environmental regulations of the country of origin.

Impression number   10 9 8 7 6 5 4 3
Year   2010 2009 2008

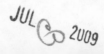

contents

Thanks to Joolz for giving me the idea for this in the first place.

Thanks to my family for putting up with me all these years.

introduction

The only assumption I shall make of you, the reader, is that you know nothing about making a film.

This book is a concise, honest, I hope humorous and straightforward guide for those of you who are desperate to make a film but feel held back since you haven't a clue how or where to start. Whether you wish to make a simple film about you and some friends or something on a larger scale, then read on. This book does not waffle on about 'ciné-verité' in the post-war era but deals exclusively with the important and practical issues.

What I hope to outline is that almost anyone can make a film. I appreciate that the film industry, despite its perpetual allure, still appears somewhat aloof and mysterious and seems a difficult industry to become a part of. I hope that after reading this book the process of making a film will be considerably demystified.

My own varied experience of making films and working in TV has provided me with the kind of knowledge that can cost thousands to hear from a film and TV consultancy. Beware some of the confusing nonsense saying you can be the next Steven Spielberg, written by someone who's more interested in selling their expensive book from the adverts in the back of your favourite film mag, than actually telling you anything useful. Don't be drawn into spending silly amounts on some bogus film course run by charlatans who cram 50 or so people into their 'schools' and then leave them to fight over a single obsolete TV camera from 1974 that doesn't work.

With this book, it is my intention to show you that making a film isn't some arcane art shrouded in the mists of secrecy, but a very straightforward process, if you just take it step-by-step.

Now let's get on with making your first feature film.

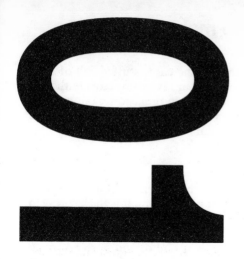

01

getting ready

In this chapter you will learn:
- what components you need to obtain
- the qualities you need to exercise
- what general attributes you need to consider.

What you need to make a feature-length film

No, you don't need several attaché cases stuffed full of used notes, or the phone numbers of your favourite actors (although it would help). The things you need in order to set out on your quest to make a film are much more rudimentary, and a mixture of personal qualities and physical bits and pieces.

1 A script

This is very important as it will be a great help if you have a story or finished script that you wish to film. It is the key way in which you can show people what you want to do, what the plot is and who the characters are. You can highlight parts in the script that you are exceptionally proud of and bore people to death with them. Basically, it's the first building block in the arduous task of making a film. If there's no script there are no characters and no story. You've got nothing to film. It would be like arranging a birthday party and then realizing that you don't know anyone who is having a birthday. A script is the source of your film. It is the plan for the whole venture. Even if you haven't a clue about anything else, you will at least be able to show others what your 'blueprint' looks like.

2 A telephone

You will have to contact a large number of people and organizations as you get things moving. These may range from friends who will take part in the film, to camera hire organizations and places where you want to film. A phone will therefore be your front line of communication. A fax would be a help as well. Did you know that some production companies for TV shows and films are nothing more than a producer and a secretary in a dingy office? And guess what – they've all got phones!

3 A word processor

Although we all live in the digital, computer age I doubt every single prospective film maker out there will have a word processor. Fear not, as you probably have a friend somewhere who can help you out here. Failing that, a local school, college or community group will have this equipment, and you should be able to come to some sort of arrangement with them. So get on that *phone*, and arrange something!

But why do I need a word processor?

In the course of phoning people to tell them about your script, whether it's the local under-16 drama group or Jean Luc Besson, they will invariably ask for you to send them preliminary details in writing. These details should take the form of a word-processed letter or email, and not a scrawl of purple crayon on the back of a beer mat. Sending a word-processed or typed letter will show that you are professional and serious about what you want to do. (I've received handwritten letters from prospective film makers asking for production money and they didn't look great.) These letters will be read by people and groups who may never have seen you before and a typed letter will create a good first impression of you and the project.

A useful hint here is to make some letter headed paper with your production company's name on it and, maybe, a logo. (More about this later.)

4 Audacity and ingenuity

When making a film, depending on its complexity and your ambition, you will probably have to call up complete strangers in various organizations and businesses to ask for some outrageous and cheeky favours and assistance.

I once produced a film set in 1987 Czechoslovakia where several scenes in my script were set in a Czech pub. I had to find out whether there was a Czech beer company operating nearby, so I went to my local supermarket and looked for some Czech beer. When I found that they stocked some, I went to the customer service desk and asked for the number of the supermarket's head office. I called up the number and asked for the department that dealt with purchasing alcohol. When I was connected I asked them if they could give me the number of the company that marketed the Czech beer, and then called that number. I got through to the head honcho, explained to him that I was making a film set in Czechoslovakia and asked if he could he help. To cut a long story short I was given thousands of pounds' worth of beer, props and technical assistance. Film sponsorship from the aisles of the local supermarket! Although I didn't actually get any cash, the support I was given put me in good stead for when I approached funding bodies (the National Lottery) – about which I'll talk later. If you don't ask, you don't get.

5 Motivation and determination

No one is forcing you to make your first film and if you want to achieve something it's up to you how hard to try. Things won't always go to plan, and it's your call whether you want to go on or quit when things turn pear shaped. It's by no means easy, but the more you put into something, the more you get out of it.

6 Confidence

This is a personal quality you need if you are to get anywhere. There's no point trying to get a project as large as a feature film, or perhaps a five- or ten-minute short, off the ground with a negative attitude. Keep your chin up and go for it! Even when you seem to be facing a string of disasters, carry on and keep going for it!

7 Be organized

Despite the apparent glamour of working in the film and television industry, a huge percentage of the job is given over to the rather dull task of administration. A film is a very fiddly exercise in managing various pieces of information required to make the project. If you can't keep track of things (how many will depend on the size of the project) you will not go far.

As the project progresses you will be receiving, sending out and otherwise dealing with some fairly large amounts of information. These might include replies to your enquiries, the contact details of places and organizations that could assist you, camera rental services, drama groups and so on *ad infinitum*. If you are not careful you could soon be lost under a pile of little bits of paper and Post-it notes with phone numbers and people's names written all over them. And sooner or later you are going to have to get in contact with these people again and call them up to arrange a meeting or send them further details. I've been in film production offices which looked like ransacked stationery retailers – this is what happens when people aren't organized.

I'm not saying that you have to rush out and buy the latest office equipment or enrol on a management course at the local night school, but it is important to sort out some system that allows you to know exactly where a piece of information is when you need it.

A simple system is to use boxes: place copies of letters asking for assistance in one, the contact details of all the places you wish to call eventually in another, and copies of the script in another. Just make sure you keep the subjects separate before you are overwhelmed by a heap of paper. For example, don't just have one stack of details, or soon you will discover that the phone number of the guy who said he could loan you the cameras for free is lost somewhere under the monster on your desk or floor.

A lever arch file with coloured paper separator sheets seems to be the industry norm these days. It's up to you; a little common sense is all you need here.

8 Free time

There's a huge number of things to do when planning a film and you will need considerable free time if you are to achieve it all. Obviously, if you have a job or are in full-time education you could try arranging things in your lunch hour. However, guess what? The people you want to speak to will probably be at lunch as well! The same goes for calling people at weekends. (I've known people who've tried to arrange projects by calling at off-peak times only, in order to save money, but these projects never got far.)

I'm not saying it's impossible, but it does mean that you will be under a lot of pressure from your work *and* from your endeavours to get your baby airborne. The solution is to have a friend, or friends, who are very, very, very excited and interested in the film idea who have the spare time to help you out. However, be expected to help them out with regard to the costs of mailing and faxing things, because they may not have the money to do it all the time! As the saying goes: a problem shared is a problem halved.

9 Nerves of steel (or at least tensile copper)

By now you should be in the process of realizing that there are a lot of things to take into consideration. More importantly, if you do things right, your mind will be juggling lots and lots of information: timetables for filming, getting in contact with people, sending replies to people and organizations, keeping people informed and so on, and that's before you've even started filming. Depending on the intended size of your film, the responsibility of handling all these aspects can get a little intense. If you don't think you can handle it, then you shouldn't start in the first place.

You are the commander-in-chief of this project and, as such, you may feel at times as though your world is collapsing all about you. It's unpleasant – take my word for it – but it's of your own making and thus you must cope with it. Anyone can fold under pressure; few can focus!

10 Creativity

Many people overlook this basic principle. To make a film you have to be creative. Any film, no matter how bad, no matter how sensational or successful it may have been, was made by a creative person or persons. Are you creative? Of course you are – you're reading this book aren't you? For some reason in our modern, sterile and sometimes harsh world, creativity is something that is frowned upon. Never be ashamed of this talent – it marks you out as different from huge swathes of the population. Express this quality you have and do something with it – you may even be able to make some money, or an entire career, from it.

11 A camera

Rather obvious really, but more on this later.

12 People

More on this later.

That's quite a few things to take into consideration isn't it? So, do you still wish to continue? (By the way, did you notice that I didn't mention any formal qualifications?)

02

script writing

In this chapter you will learn:
- what it takes to form a story
- the 'formula' of popular script writing
- the overall format for presenting a script.

In this chapter we shall be looking at the processes that will take you from the point of your story's conception to your script's unveiling. As highlighted in the previous chapter, you need to have completed your script, or at least have some defined idea about it, before you can start producing in earnest.

The story line

It is very important to consider what your story will be about. Perhaps time-travelling cowboys, or a period piece à la Jane Austen, or an experimental political commentary?

Basically, the decision is yours. The only person who should have a say on whether your ideas and script are any good is *you*. My golden rule when I'm writing is: 'If I like it, then it's good!' That's what you should be aiming for. Everyone is different, and films and all other aspects of creative art reflect this. I mean, I love the film *The Empire Strikes Back*, I think it's one of the best stories that will ever exist, but my aunt thinks the same of *The Sound of Music*. Two very different films, yet both very popular and enduring. You could be influenced commercially when you finally sit down to compose the first draft of your script, or you might just want to write something that makes sense to you. That's perfectly fine.

Developing characters

There are, of course, a few constants that you will have to get right if you are to get your script off the ground, regardless of your 'ultimate vision'. One of these is your characters. All words spoken as dialogue will utter forth from the mouth of one of your imagined beings. An easy way to get going is to play around with a set number – three, for example – and to think of a character for each number. How do they relate to each other? What is their history? Why are they in your script? What do they do? Are they male or female, the goodie or baddie?

By doing this you can start forming ideas in your mind from which greater things will grow. You may feel that three characters is too small a number, but it is a nice mid-point to start with for the purpose of illustrating the point I'm making. Once this has been decided, it may be useful to put it down on paper in chart form. I don't really like putting literary things into chart form – as per Robin Williams' character in the *Dead Poets Society*, during the page-tearing-out scene – but for the purposes of helping you, here goes:

Character	Occupation	Personality	Age	Reason for being in film
Richard Vincent	Private detective	Cool, sharp, treacherous	34	Finds a suitcase full of money
Ellie Mahonie	Glamorous lady	Mysterious, silent	29	Says she's lost a large amount of money
Mr Vittorio	Mr Vincent's assistant	Nervous, clumsy	45	Helps out Richard Vincent

and so on…

So you see that Richard Vincent is a man, he works as a private detective and he's in the film because he's found a suitcase full of money. He's cool, sharp and a little treacherous.

Ellie Mahonie is a woman, she's glamorous and she's in the film because she claims she's lost the money. She's mysterious and doesn't say much.

Mr Vittorio is a man, he's Richard Vincent's assistant and he's in the film because he's helping out his boss Richard. He's nervous and clumsy.

Now that the characters are sorted out, one word of essential advice is to keep the characters consistent. I've seen many scripts where the characters not only change personalities, but after page 10 undergo a name change. It happens all the time when a character starts off as a mean, tough, gun-toting cop and a few pages later he's a bit of a pushover and doesn't really care about much. This is usually because the writer has run out of steam and hasn't thought about the story or what is going on in the head of the characters he/she has just created.

Try to get it into your head that the dialogue that you will eventually be writing is not *really* coming from you, but from the mouths of people! Therefore, the words will be spouting out from different people, not just headers on the page that state names.

Setting

So, with the above three examples of characters in mind, you can start thinking about a setting. The characters here could easily inhabit a sleazy, city underworld full of danger and excitement, as opposed to running a veterinary practice on the Isle of Lewis in Iceland. Characters and setting come from the same primordial soup – they are symbiots of each other – and this is worth remembering when you are 'populating' your world. They are *acting* and *reacting* to each other.

Put together, characters and setting have got to do something. The characters do things in the setting. They interact with the other people in the script and with the lesser individual who makes an appearance for only one line. Don't just have them hanging around reading newspapers all day long – there's a story that's pushing and pulling them over each page of your script. These aren't just words, it's an exciting marathon where anything can happen. It's all up to you.

All right, so a pushing story for Mr Richard Vincent and his pals is the fact that he's found some stolen cash; Ellie Mahonie says it belongs to her and Mr Vittorio is trying to help his boss. So what's going to happen? Here is one possible scenario.

Richard Vincent is in his office when he receives a mysterious phone call asking him to help out a pal of his on the other side of town. He arrives at the rendezvous and discovers that there's been a big shoot-out and lots of people are lying dead on the floor, including his pal. He sees a case full of cash, which he takes, then leaves before the police come. He stashes the money in a bank and coolly sits tight.

A couple of days later he's in his office again and he gets a phone call from a woman who says she needs Mr Vincent's help. She asks him to meet her in a bar. Before he goes, he tells his assistant that he's found a case of cash and that it's in a certain bank. Before Mr Vittorio can ask more, Richard leaves.

Richard meets up in the bar with the woman who says her name is Ellie Mahonie and that she's lost a great deal of money. She asks if he can help her out. Without telling her of his find the other day, he says he'll have a go and try to locate it for her. Next day Richard Vincent and Mr Vittorio go to the bank to check out the money. Richard realizes that so much money might draw attention, so he changes some of it into traveller's cheques (and why not?). Mr Vittorio is anxious to know how much is left, but Richard Vincent doesn't tell him, mentioning that it's safer if he doesn't know any more about it.

Later on he phones Ellie from his office and tells her that he reckons the money is long gone by now. He lies and says he tried everywhere and asked all the sources but that the 'word on the street' is that it's vanished. Ellie is distraught and hangs up on him. Richard knows the money's not his, and feels a bit bad, but he's made his choice... DRAMATIC MUSIC!

What will happen next? It doesn't take a huge amount of effort to roll a story idea around in your head. The more you play with the characters, setting and overall story you've decided upon, the easier it becomes.

Writing is a really important part of the film-making process and it will help a director a great deal if he/she can write. It's the best way to get to grips with the mechanics of your story.

As Francis Ford Coppola said to a young George Lucas:

'If you want to direct... you've got to write.'

However, if you want to take your script to production companies and the like, they may be more inclined to listen to someone who has written a Hollywood-flavoured film as opposed to a gritty social drama set in a housing estate in Leeds. So saying, who could have guessed *The Full Monty* would be such a success? Remember, you are the creator, so decide what you want, stick to your guns and don't let others influence you.

How long should my script be?

That again is up to you. Just because you are setting out on a creative process as big as a film need not mean that the script has to be the size of the local phone directory. The professional rule of thumb for film timing is: 1 page = 1 minute of film time.

When you watch a film, the characters do not speak non-stop from start to finish – there will be many scenes were no one is speaking and these scenes add length to the film which isn't always highlighted clearly in a script. If you were to read the script for your favourite feature-length film, and read all the lines non-stop, you would probably be done in about 45 minutes, depending on how fast you read. Size does not always equate to quality. It depends on what's on the pages!

What format should my script take?

This very much depends on your intended audience. If you want to make the film with friends, or a local non-professional group, then your only concern is to make it legible. However, if you want to be taken seriously or want a big and famous company to take a look at it, then it has to be done in a certain way, an example of which is shown below.

Scene 12

EXT. High Street, Bank - Day
It is raining and a black Cadillac pulls up. Mr Vittorio and Richard get out, look around the street and slowly make their way into the bank. Mr Vittorio opens the door and whispers to Richard.

Mr Vittorio
Are you sure you want to do this?
Richard unbuttons his tatty coat.

Richard
Yes, get a move on.

INT. Bank - Day
Richard and Mr Vittorio enter the bank foyer and make their way to a free cashier.

Mr Vittorio
(nervous)
Couldn't we wait for the rest of the crew?

Richard
Put a lid on it!

They approach the cashier. Mr Vittorio is looking nervously about the interior of the bank.

Richard puts his gloved hand into his unbuttoned coat.

Richard
I'd like some traveller's cheques please.

Cashier
Certainly, Sir, do you have any identification?

Richard extracts his passport from his inner coat pocket.

The professional rule of thumb for script format is:

- Twelve-point courier text on A4 paper (i.e. size 12, courier style from the word processor, as per the script example on page 12).
- Speech text to be indented by two spaces or centre justified.
- Character names to be indented by three spaces, or centre justified, and marked in **bold**.
- 'Exterior' and 'interior' should be abbreviated in bold to '**EXT.**' or '**INT.**' and should appear immediately before explanatory text.
- *Don't* write camera moves into the script (e.g. zoom in, pan along) – that's what the director does after he or she has read the script, plus it muddles the script and the reader.

(A television and film writer once shared the above pointers with me and then, quite rightly, said he couldn't understand how there's a whole sub-industry in books and courses based around those five points!)

The script example opposite is quite basic, but I hope it gives you a good idea of the general format. By the way, how would you have filmed that? You could have kept it quick and to the point, or you could have drawn it out into a suspense-filled set piece dripping with colour and danger. As I mentioned earlier, the number of words in a script can have little bearing on the final length of the film.

Tips on script writing

So what tips can I give you here? One concept that professional script writers keep telling people is: *keep it simple*. A simple script usually has the following fundamental characteristics:

1 The number of characters is limited.

2 The locations are small in number.

3 It has a **beginning** (where the story, setting and characters are introduced).

4 It has a **complication** a little way into the film, when things become interesting and the adventure/story/reason for you being in the cinema begins. For example, in *Star Wars* this is when Luke's uncle buys the two robots, one of which has information about the baddies and the image of the princess they need to rescue. If he had bought another pair, the adventure and story would have stopped there and then.

Another classic example of this is in the film *Witness*, starring Harrison Ford and Kelly McGillis. A few minutes into the film the Amish woman and her young boy are in a busy train station. While the young boy is in one of the toilet cubicles he witnesses a murder. Now if that boy hadn't gone to the toilet, then he wouldn't have seen the murder, he wouldn't be the witness and there would be no film. Think about some of your favourite films to see where this complication is. It's not always that apparent, but it's there, and without that one simple action there would be no film.

5 It also has a **middle**, when the story falls into its pace. A few other characters may get thrown in, a few adventures develop and scrapes happen, and ultimately it legitimizes the ending. The middle of the film comes soon or immediately after the moment of complication. Using the example of *Star Wars* again, it's when Luke goes off with Ben and the droids and meets Han and Chewie. They outrun the Empire, end up in the Death Star, have a few fights with the baddies and then try to escape.

In *Gladiator* it's after Maximus has been betrayed by his soldiers and the dastardly Commodus and has to escape from Germany, gets caught by the slave traders, trains as a gladiator, has loads of fights and comes up with his plan to take command of his army again.

Even a non-action film like the *Dead Poets Society* keeps to the trend: after the complication (when Robin Williams' character appears) the story goes into its cruise mode with the students involved in the adventure of discovering literature, Shakespeare and creativity.

6 It then has a **second complication**. This is the bridge that links the middle and the end. Going back once more to the example of *Star Wars*, the second complication here is when Han, Chewie, Princess Leia, Luke and the droids escape from the Death Star which takes them directly to the big battle at the end of the film. In *Gladiator*, the second complication is when Maximus's plot to escape from Rome and join up with his army has been foiled, which takes him to the showdown with Commodus. Even *Dead Poets Society* has it, when one of the students kills himself. It's just a formula.

7 Finally it has an **ending** (when the events after the second complication are resolved). The ending of the film is when all the contents of the film come to a head and are in some way resolved. Without an ending the story would just go on and

on. Some films resolve matters better than others. A popular resolving scenario is when there is a huge shoot-out and the baddies get killed amidst huge explosions, crashing cars, earthquakes and so on.

The climax of the whole story often ends up as a major set piece where all the elements of the film (the characters and the story, for example, the baddie's HQ where the kidnapped girl is being held who has been a focus of the film so far) are in the same place, and it is just a great method to wrap things up rather conveniently.

Tango and Cash illustrates very well the 'big bang' way of resolving a film. Have you ever wondered why this method is so popular? Bascially, it is a very easy way of sorting things out. The film has got loads of baddies crawling out of the woodwork. They're all after the good guy, so how can the film be wrapped up? Easy. Kill all the baddies. It's convenient, it's clean, it leaves the hero free to walk off into the sunset while triumphant music plays. I'm sure you can think of many, many examples of the above. However, this 'rule' isn't always adhered to. Sometimes the heroes are killed, for example, in *Thelma and Louise*. We don't actually see them being killed, but it is an assumption the audience is supposed to make. In *Gladiator*, Maximus dies at the end of the film. Again this brings a definite close to the proceedings, and though sad to some, it ends the film very well.

Have you ever watched a film and felt a bit ambivalent about the ending, as if the film is not quite finished? The expected foreclosure is not there. When I watched *The Empire Strikes Back* as a youngster, I thought the film was going to continue as Lando and Chewie flew off. The story hadn't been resolved, things were still up in the air, it didn't make sense. At the time I was unaware of the workings of sequels.

Unresolved films tend to be unsuccessful, perhaps because the audience is a bit peeved that the story has been left dangling in the air somewhere. When you have thought about the characters, setting and basic story, it may be a good idea to jot down a time-line with the above 'events' along it. The complication will usually appear a third of the way in, the second complication about one third from the end, with the adventure/middle falling between the two. You can play around with your story in this form without having to rewrite whole pages. Just scribble down what the complication is, what happens during the adventure/middle and what the key events are and what form the ending takes. Try it, you'll be amazed at how liberating this method can be (see Figure 1).

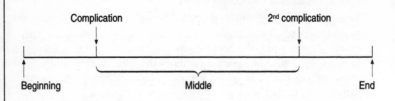

figure 1

The 'keep it simple' principle is a great starting point for many film makers. I heard some of this when I was watching a documentary about the making of *Reservoir Dogs*. Although the film is based on the Hong Kong film *City of Fire*, it was translated by Tarantino in a relatively stripped down, no frills way. Most of the characters are killed before they've had a chance to say much (and thus pick up smaller pay cheques) and a large proportion of the film takes place in the warehouse. Essentially, you could argue that *Reservoir Dogs* is a film about three people arguing in a large room. Simple.

Cult horror films often follow the same formula. They usually start off with some teenagers driving through the wilderness. The car breaks down and one of them says, 'Hey, let's stay the night in that old house over there', and the rest of the film takes place in the house. We've all seen them. It is worth bearing in mind that simple ideas will not incur the same hassles as a Hollywood epic such as *Spartacus*.

Another great feature of the 'keep it simple' way of thinking is that you can get a 'less is more' effect out of the dialogue. Many people who sit down and write their first script have a tendency to write huge chunks of dialogue every time a character speaks. Don't make your scripts too wordy. Next time you watch a film, notice that the characters don't tend to say a great deal every time they speak – maybe one or two sentences. So don't think that you need to compose a page of elegant prose each time a character says something.

When thinking about your script and film, bounce some story ideas around in your head. Not all successful film makers write the screenplays to their films, but instead think up the story and recruit someone else to write it. Next time you watch the opening credits to a film you might see the following:

Screenplay by Mr X

Based on a story by Mrs Y

Thinking up ideas is easy, all it requires is letting your mind drift for a while. It usually works well with two people who are throwing ideas at each other. Eventually an idea will be finalized and you'll say: 'OK, this is it. Man gets arrested for bank robbery, is taken to prison, starts having dreams about being abducted by aliens, finds out his clone did the robbery, uses hidden power to break out of prison, looks for aliens, gives them a good kicking, then becomes a manager of a restaurant.' Voilà!

Using other works

Look at other films, plays and books and use their ideas – thievery keeps the film world alive – but don't plagiarize. As mentioned above, Tarantino used *City of Fire*; the entry of the spacecraft in *Independence Day* was a rip-off from the first few pages of the Arthur C. Clarke novel *Childhood's End* (although the film's producers may argue differently); *Bladerunner* is styled on a Humphrey Bogart detective film set in the future; the scrolling introduction and political situation in *Star Wars* is taken straight from Roman history books after the death of Julius Caesar, and so on. From your observation of films and books it should not take a huge amount of mental energy to think of a famous or obscure story you would like to alter for the purposes of writing a script. However, try not to make it too obvious, but be subversive, change names, setting, the time and so on.

Finally, when you do write the script, keep it in the **present tense**. Novels are written mostly in the past; scripts are written in the present. So let's compare the same story written in script and novel formats.

Novel format

Richard Vincent slowly opened the glass door of the bar and wiped the cold rain from his tattered coat. His face was hidden under his large trilby as he peered about the dark, smoky innards of the bar, looking for the woman who had called him here.

A few drunk faces made eye contact with him as he stood inert in the doorway. The rest slurped away at the cheap spirits and beer as they half sat, half slouched at their tables or on bar stools.

He took off his hat slowly and threw it on to the nearby hatstand.

'Hey, Mack!' shouted the bar tender, 'are you gonna order anything, or just drip all over my floor?' Richard looked over at the burly man and smiled curtly.

'Jerk,' whispered Richard, and then made his way across the room.

As he sat down, he reached into his inner pocket and pulled out a packet of cigarettes and put one to his mouth.

'Allow me,' said a soft female voice. Richard looked to his left and saw the face of the woman he was looking for. She lit his Marlboro.

'Sure,' he replied coolly.

'I thought you'd never come,' she said, eyeing the bottles racked up behind the bar.

'Well, I got nothing better to do,' he mumbled nonchalantly.

The heavy steps of the bartender echoed over the floor behind the bar as he walked up to Richard and the woman.

'So, what'll it be?'

'I'll have,' began Richard.

'Two large bourbons, straight up,' said the woman, smiling, with her eyes on Richard.

Script format

```
INT. Gionetti's Bar, Downtown - Night
The dimly lit bar is thick with smoke. A few
people are sitting at tables or drinking at
the bar. The glass door to the bar opens and
Richard Vincent enters. He stands in the
doorway and wipes the rain from his tatty
coat. He takes off his wide-brimmed hat and
throws it on a nearby hat stand.
                    Bartender
          (shouting to Richard)
```

> Hey Mack, are you gonna order anything or just drip all over my floor?

                          Richard
>   (aside)
>   Jerk!

Richard makes his way to the bar and sits down. He pulls out a packet of cigarettes and puts one in his mouth. A woman suddenly sits down to his left.

                          Woman
>   Allow me.

She lights his cigarette.

                          Richard
>   Sure.

                          Woman
>   I thought you'd never come.

                          Richard
>   Well, I got nothing better to do.

The bartender walks up to the pair.

                          Bartender
>   So, what'll it be?

                          Richard
>   I'll have...

                          Woman
>   (looking at Richard)
>   Two large bourbons, straight up.

See the difference? In a nutshell, a script is less descriptive than text in novel form.

A novelist describes situations with *words*. A film maker does it with *pictures*!

I personally find it's easier to write things in script form, so have a go yourself. Try having a look at some passages from your favourite book and then rewriting it in script format. Pretty soon you'll get the hang of it. Since the script content is such an enormously subjective thing, I'll leave you to decide how to write yours. Just remember to follow the basic format and story rules. Use your imagination, have fun and see you later.

Bottom-line rules of script writing

- Make sure that your story is well formed before you start to write the script.

- If you feel comfortable with the concept, then stick to the 'keep it simple' guidelines.

- Try to keep the characters consistent, and remember that they are 'real' people.

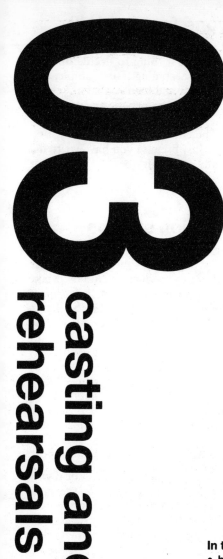

03

casting and rehearsals

In this chapter you will learn:
- how to talk about and verbally present your idea
- how to co-ordinate first moves towards assembling a cast
- how to iron out problems and avoid troublesome people.

Script! Script! Anyone for a script?

Now that you have finished your script, you need to interest other people interested in it. The first thing to decide upon is how big you see this idea of yours becoming. For example, is it going to be a film made with friends and Dad's camcorder, or a low-key local film involving local drama groups and technical personnel poached from local colleges, or do you see it as next summer's blockbuster? The choice, once again, is yours. However, you must be realistic. Just because you have written a script that you are exceptionally proud of does not mean that MGM studios will be calling you for a chat.

Approaching production studios

If your ambitions do lie along these lines then you will prepare lots of copyrighted copies, or a page-long synopsis, otherwise known as a **treatment**, to send out to production studios. Make sure you call the studios up first to explain what the script is about, otherwise you may send your script for *Rambo 4* to a place that only makes films about animal husbandry. If you do choose this route, then be prepared to wait a long time for replies, and bear in mind that production companies get literally thousands of scripts every year, each one written and sent in by someone like you with their eyes on making a fortune. Don't always expect a favourable reply, or a reply at all! I'm not saying it's impossible for your dreams to come true, but it is damned hard. You may have to call up every production company and film studio in the world before someone finally says, 'I'm interested'. Even then, this may well be the limit of their support.

However, beware of the ways in which these big places deal with the multitude of submissions that are sent to them by the truck load on a weekly basis. The same fellow who mentioned the script format pointers to me, also told me of his experiences as a reader. As the name suggests, a reader reads scripts to determine whether they have the potential to make a great film or are complete rubbish. Most of the scripts that are sent in are binned or, if the company has enough money, posted back to the writer or writer's agent.

On his first day of employment with the script-reading agency, the reader's boss said: '*Your job is to make the sofa into a mattress.*' All the scripts that had been sent in had been arranged into a makeshift sofa capable of seating several people at a time. The reader's job was to work his way through them all, finding the good ones. (The Orange cinema trailers, where stars have their film ideas ruined, shows the main producer sitting on a chair made of submitted scripts.)

Bearing in mind the quantity of scripts that production companies and reading agencies receive, it is impossible to read every single one from start to finish – it would take far too long. If a story doesn't jump out by page 10 (or earlier) the script is usually thrown away. It is therefore imperative to make your story interesting early on. This doesn't just apply to submitting your film script, but also to making the film.

Your submission needs to convey a story and plot line that will hook people. It may be hard to achieve the right formula to get the **hook**, but it is one of the things that will make the story (and consequent film) interesting and, it's hoped, original. In short, find some names, phone them, pay for lots of postage, send the scripts out... and wait.

Going it alone

Now, for those of you who are impatient, don't give a hoot for all those big fancy film-making places or simply like going it alone, then it's much easier to interest people in the project. Besides, this book is about *you* making *your* film, not someone else doing it for you!

Your first port of call will probably be within a few miles of your front door. Think about people or organizations who might be interested in acting out your script. You could try the local dramatics society, the school acting group, a local performing arts college and certainly your friends.

Look them up in the phone book and call them. In the case of the local drama society, they will usually be happy for you to turn up and talk about your ideas. No doubt some will be fascinated by your script, others may consider it beneath them *daaarling*. Make sure, however, that you are approaching the right type of groups; your *Reservoir Dogs* rip-off script won't sit well with the drama group of the local kindergarten, for example.

Setting the pitch

Some of these groups or individuals may ask for written details of the intended production so they can consider it. It is therefore a good idea and a professional courtesy to have a treatment ready to give these people to provide them with some basic details of the story and so forth. In addition to the treatment/synopsis it is vital to figure out what your verbal **pitch** is. For example, when you speak to people who may be able to help you, on the phone or at meetings, they may ask for some primary verbal details. Discussing the entire script may be a bit time consuming for some people, so instead you pitch the idea to them. You hit them with what I term the 'story bullet' (more commonly called the pitch). The entire film is compressed into a few sentences which you can fire off at people as and when needed so that someone is 'hit' with an immediate idea of what the story is about.

'A kid goes back in time to save his parent's marriage', is how one Hollywood executive recalled the pitch for *Back to the Future*. Think of a few films and practise making up your own pitches. Even the most complicated films can be condensed to a concise pitch.

An even shorter variant of the pitch is the 'high concept' of a film. An example of two high concepts I have used is '*Hornblower* meets *Amistad*' when talking about an idea for a film script about a slave who ends up as a sailor in the Royal Navy and serves on the *HMS Victory* at the Battle of Trafalgar. Another was '*Bill and Ted* meets *James Bond – The Living Daylights*' when drumming up interest in my Czechoslovakian-themed film.

The high concept is a very effective way to implant a sudden mental image in someone's head without having to endlessly explain things. The best high concept I ever heard was '*Lord of the Rings* in space' for the original Star Wars trilogy.

In television it is just the same. When phoning up hundreds of groups and organizations in the pre-production for a drama or documentary, one of the first things people fire off is the pitch or high concept so the person at the other end is suddenly hit with a mental image of what is being planned. This may sound like a less than major point, but I have seen film makers who, when asked about their film, have looked back wide eyed and have been quite unable to articulate themselves in less than several minutes.

Getting back to the actors: it's important to be realistic with them – just as it is with yourself. Don't tell them that you'll make them famous or make them rich (you may not even be able to pay them!). Tell them what's what and don't lead them up the garden path.

Rehearsals

Arrange somewhere to rehearse. It doesn't have to be anywhere special; it could be at your house, at a community centre, at a youth club, or in a room at a school. Although this may be your first time directing a rehearsal, try not to panic. Remember, it's your script and your idea the people have come about, so try to be cool.

Arrange a preliminary workshop/read-through of the script, making sure that you have the contact details of those who you want to come along, to help ensure they turn up. Send out the parts of the script, or the whole thing, to their addresses or give it to them on the day. Make sure they known where and when the meeting is to be held.

One of the 'between the lines' elements of making films and being a director is that you have to get on with a wide variety of people who will look to you as their leader. Although this may be nerve-racking, try to look vaguely serious about what is going on – even though it could be a zany comedy you've written – as it will make it clear that you are committed to the project. Remember, these people don't *have* to be here, they are giving up free time to help you out!

The first read-through is a time when things either make sense or they don't. Basically it's the test drive. As the writer, it's up to you to make any necessary changes. A character giving a beautiful soliloquy while full of bullet holes may work on paper, but when it's being read out in the context of the situation it may look ridiculous. After the first read-through you should know what needs to be done to the script (if anything), who is most suited to the roles and who is not suited to anything. Just because you have got people reading out lines, doesn't mean they will fit the part.

Don't be too set in your ideas about what your characters will look like, as most of the time such a person will not be at your auditions or rehearsals. You may find that you are completely surprised by someone who turns up and reads for you, so don't write a part thinking that the person who plays it should look like someone out of your favourite film or you may find yourself on a hopeless quest. It's part of the casting process and you need someone who fits your *idea* about who the character is, so try to keep an open mind.

An example of the above was when I was looking for two men to read the parts of two hippy/bum/idiot students. I must have heard at least ten hopefuls and it just didn't work. Then one day a guy who looked like Billy Idol was paired with a tall red-haired man who looked like he was a Confederate army recruit – and it worked like a dream. So who knows?

Use a video

It is always a good idea to try to video your rehearsals whenever possible. Not only does this give you, as the director, the resource to play back performances to assess them and think of new ideas, but it also gets the actors used to acting in front of cameras. Some people who turn up at rehearsals may be 'first timers', while others will be seasoned drama performers, but regardless of their pedigree not everyone gets on with cameras in the same way. Some actors may be very aware and conscious of being filmed, and this can seriously compromise their performance. It is not unknown for great stage actors to freeze the first time a camera is put on them. So get everyone used to having cameras follow their every move. Not only will this help your actors, but it is a great way to practise using your chosen camera (see later). Think of it as a school where you will be trying out different camera effects and techniques, choreographing your scenes, anticipating problems you may encounter while filming, and practising framing (see later).

With each rehearsal things will get better. If they don't, it usually means one of two things:

1 You haven't fully explained the characters, the background to the story, or some aspect of the script.
2 You have a troublemaker amidst your ranks.

The former isn't too difficult to clear up; the latter takes a bit more mettle. A troublemaker is usually a person who, for reasons only known to themselves, is intent on ruining your parade. They manifest themselves in different ways. They may want to change things in the script, such as the story and characters; they may want to be the main focus of the story, even though they have only one line; or they refuse to co-operate with the rest of the actors and yourself.

Whatever the reason, the solution is to show them the door. It's something you've got to do, and if you leave it too late your film could become a mess. This is a factor that shouldn't be overlooked as it can sometimes rear its very ugly head and turn your film into an unpleasant chore. There will always be, of course, moments during a read-through when suggestions will be thrown in by everyone, and you should be sensitive to these pointers. The whole point of the readings is to hammer out any problems, *but*, don't be rail-roaded into completely changing your script into something you don't want it to be. There are people who seem to think that it's a free-for-all where they can enter into the group and start sticking their unpleasant oars in. On these occasions, act fast, otherwise you'll gradually be pushed out of your own creation.

Don't forget that although you are embarking on a film, you are also embarking on a 'people' project. What you are planning and doing will eventually consist of people. This is something that sometimes scares many 'reclusive' potential film directors who have sweated out their script while locked away in their bedroom. When things have started to get going, such people have been terrified at the prospect that they will actually be dealing with people who are the vital ingredients in their film making recipe.

This is the great unwritten component of making films. You have to speak to and get on with many different people – be they potential contributors on the other end of a telephone, or people at auditions and rehearsals. Invariably many of these people will be rather creative (difficult) and it will be up to you to prevent them from getting out of control and becoming the director, and instead simply saying the lines as you want them to.

The rehearsal process is the great testing ground for this quality in a director. You will be confronted by a variety of people, some you will know, some you won't. The sight of several faces looking at you and your script is rather daunting, but just try to relax and take the problems and issues one at a time.

The first things to establish, if you haven't already done so, is who is reading for which part, what scenes you will be going through (things may not be at a stage to read the whole script), what order you will be doing things in and what props you will be using (tables, chairs, toy guns etc.).

Again, this goes back to being organized. Having a timetable of where and when rehearsals will take place, will go a long way to show people that you are organized, and it will also let everyone know what the order of the rehearsals will be.

Once the preliminary order of events has been established, just have a read-through of whatever scenes you are able to do and take stock of what is going on, for example, what people sound like, whether people are getting the context of the scene right, whether the idea is getting across, whether the accents are believable and so on. As the writer of the words, you are listening to the 'play-back' and only you can really advise people what needs to be tweaked and changed.

> Don't just observe what's going on during rehearsals. Direct it!

Don't forget, a *director* gives *direction*. Although this may seem a bit of a basic observation, many people forget this, or are too worried about raising their voices and actually directing a group of energetic and creative individuals. Don't just sit back and take in what is going on before you, explain things to people, tell them how and why this character speaks in the way he does. It is all too easy to listen to a scene that is read in a manner that makes your blood curdle and then at the end of it say, 'Yeah, that was great. OK, let's read the next one,' for the sake of worrying that you may upset someone. You won't if you explain things in a diplomatic manner.

It is very easy to forget that the people attending the read-throughs and rehearsals do not share your sense of empathy and 'oneness' with the script. Only you have that 'power', and it is wrong to expect everyone to get the picture as soon as they start reading what is front of them. Things will need explaining... just be patient in your explanations. If something isn't coming together in the way that you absolutely want it to, then make an effort to correct it before it gets lost amidst the frenetic energy and chaos of your rehearsals.

This harks back to the section on writing the script. Since you have thought of the characters, you know what is pushing and driving them, so you should impart those details to the potential cast members as and when the situation requires it. Remember that some of the people who turn up at these rehearsals and read-throughs can be very precise with their methods. Simply having a name on a script followed by sections of speech will not be enough to propel them on through the odyssey of your film making foray. And remember the other section on writing your script: these characters are 'real people', they have reasons for doing things, they have personalities, they are, above all, characters in *your* world. As the scriptwriter you have the intrinsic knowledge and ability to explain *everything* about the script you have created. So once again, the script isn't just a jumble of words, names and events, it is a story that has a reason for being (no matter how bizarre you may think it is), so be prepared to explain it now and again when someone needs a bit of help figuring out why their character is the way it is. This is another of the great unstated necessities of film making: hone your vision before you are anywhere near filming. Never expect your actors to just turn up and 'fall into' the script that you have written – rehearsals and actors that have suffered from lack of direction and explanation will come together and produce a project that is both lifeless and boring and, in some cases, not the film that the director had in mind at all.

> Don't be shy – explain your 'world' and those who inhabit it.

However, once in a while, don't be too wound up to take on board the advice and ideas that your actors may come up with during rehearsals.

Bottom-line rules of casting and rehearsals

- Be organized and approachable and make an effort to get on with everyone.
- Don't pander to people who feel it is their right to change your script.
- Make sure that everyone knows what the story is about and why their characters are the way they are.
- Don't make bad casting decisions you are unhappy with just because you don't want to upset anyone.

Remember, being a director involves people skills; this doesn't always mean that you have to please everyone all the time.

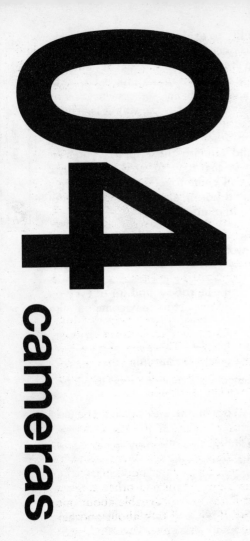

04

cameras

In this chapter you will learn:
- how to navigate the sea of modern cameras
- how to decide which camera is best suited to your production
- about the basic operating features available on video cameras.

As you might be aware, there are lots and lots of different cameras. The high-street camcorder you use to film family events is not the same system that was used to film *The English Patient*. There is a big difference, and it's important to know the kind of look certain camera systems produce.

When you watch television, you may have noticed that the images of some programmes and films have a different texture and visual quality to them. In fact, in a typical night's viewing, you will be exposed to a mixture of different camera formats ranging from cameras you can hold in your hand (obtainable from a high-street store) to huge beasts that only inhabit blockbuster films. It's a bit like different types of motorized transport – some people like getting the bus, while others have car and some own a motorbike, if you see what I'm getting at.

> Cameras fall into two main branches: video and film.

Every moving image you watch comes from a video or film image. No big news to some of you, but are you aware how those two can be further sub-divided? There are quite a few ways, but prior to entering the world of choosing what format to use, it's important not to get obsessed and concerned with high-tech gadgetry and *latest models syndrome*.

The number of formats available to you can be confusing. I remember when I was making my first film I didn't know anything about cameras, so I thought I should get out there and speak to people about all the different options. What followed was an odyssey of technical minutiae from individuals who swore by their chosen formats and rubbished other camera systems. Just when I thought I was knowledgeable about one format, someone would come along and talk about another camera system and confuse me totally. Try to stick to one format in advance, otherwise you could get lost in a labyrinth of things you really don't need to know. Too much information can be a bad thing.

Video cameras

Let's start off with a selection of video cameras. We have all seen camcorder footage. Even if you don't own a camcorder, you will have seen television programmes showing newlywed couples falling off cliffs while the audience laughs loudly. But have you ever noticed that some clips are of a much better quality than others? The reason for this is that either the camera is a super dooper one that does everything for you (apart from moving), or that the person using it knows what to do with it. The latter is what you should be aiming for.

Although camcorders are perhaps the simplest camera system to use – you just point and shoot – the quality you end up with can vary by a large margin. So, as with all camera systems, you need to know how to use it to the limit of its potential.

What camera systems are available?

Quite a few, but when you are looking at video formats in shops or colleges look out for the following features. The more of them it has, the better the camera is.

1 **White balance** This is an electronic feature that tells the camera what white is. If a camera doesn't know what white is then the footage might suffer from false colouration, for example, people's faces look jaundiced, white walls turn yellow or pale brown, natural light is hazy blue etc. This causes problems, unless you want to edit your film in black and white. Look for cameras that have this feature either as pre-sets and/or as a manual setting.

2 **Manual zoom** Having a manual zoom means your zooms can be as fast or slow as you want. If the camera doesn't have a manual zoom then you'll be stuck with rather slow zooms. The best manual zooms are on the lens barrel, but most are found as a 'rocker switch'.

3 **Manual focus** This means you can focus on whatever you want to, as opposed to what the camera decides is best (see page 124 for a fuller analysis). Like the manual zoom feature, the best manual focuses are on the lens barrel as they're easier to gauge and use, but cameras with manual focus controls elsewhere are fine – so long as it gets the job done.

4 **Manual iris/aperture controls** These control the amount of light coming into the camera, making the shot brighter or darker (see page 125 for fuller description). Like the zoom and focus, the best manual iris/aperture controls are on the lens barrel as they tend to give the user an immediacy with what they are doing, but on some cameras they are elsewhere.

5 **A microphone socket** See page 69 for the benefits of such a feature.

6 **A thread hole** This means it can be screwed to the top of a common camera tripod. However, some of the larger professional cameras mentioned in this chapter likewise require professional tripods with special 'plates' that the camera base locks into.

7 **A gain control** Gain is a function that allows you to brighten an image when there isn't enough lighting. However, be warned, the more gain you use the more grainy, rough and 'noisy' your picture will become. This can have its advantages though (see page 57 Tricks with film).

8 **A shutter speed control** Shutter speed is how fast or slowly the camera films something. Normal video camera shutter speed is 50 frames per second, but by increasing this you can impart 'flicker' on your images so that action looks heightened or more exciting. Alternatively you can have a lower shutter speed which blurs your image and makes things dreamy or haunting.

Be advised that most domestic/consumer-level camcorders won't have many of the above manual features, but instead will have them embedded within the camera's operating systems. This means they are only utilized when the *camera* thinks it needs to use them and as such they can't be accessed by the user.

So, with the above eight pointers in mind let's take a quick look at some cameras.

Video8 – 8 mm

Until relatively recently this was perhaps the most common consumer-level video camera.

It's called Video8 on account of the width of the tape cassette – 8 mm you see. It's very lightweight, which means you won't get cramp in your arm when holding it for a long time, and it also means you can swing it around for some groovy psychedelic shots. The picture quality is OK, even better if you've got good lighting on set, and the sound can be mono or stereo depending on the model. Like most other lightweight video cameras, the cassettes are cheap and are of a long duration.

Plusses:

• It was a ubiquitous format and there are still lots around that you can pick up very, very cheaply.
• Everyone has had one, so you may get one readily and cheaply second hand or else borrow one for free.

- You can easily plug it into the back of your television or video player for easy monitoring or living-room editing (see later).
- The tapes are small but you can do a lot of filming on them.

Minuses:

- It is not the greatest quality video camera in the world, that is, it is a domestic format instead of a professional/industry format.
- It can be rather limited with regards to the inclusion of the above mentioned camera features.
- You could have problems with this format if you edit on computer – see later.

VHS

As the name suggest, it uses a standard VHS cassette to record with – the type you use in your video player. Because this format uses a larger cassette, the camera is correspondingly big as well. It's big enough to rest on your shoulder so that passers by will ask you what television company you work for – a great ego boost! However, that said, there aren't many of them about anymore, apart from in under-funded colleges with media study departments or in yard sales, but this may mean you can pick one up for a very affordable price.

Plusses:

- Often regarded as semi-obsolete by many people, which means they will be cheap if you can find one.
- These cameras may possess many (if not all) of the features mentioned earlier.
- They use regular VHS tapes which can be bought anywhere – although try to get the best you can afford.
- You can play the tapes straight back on a video player, which means no juggling with leads or accidentally detuning the television.
- It is a large, sturdy thing which means it will give steadier shots when hand-held or on the shoulder.

Minuses:

- Again, like the format before, the VHS is not a professional/industry format. Therefore the visual quality is not the best there is.
- You could have problems with this format if you edit on computer – see later.

- VHS tapes are relatively large compared with others, and carrying ten of them around when filming may prove to be a bit of a chore.

S-VHS (Super VHS)

Like VHS but *super*. In simple terms, S-VHS looks a lot like a VHS camera, but it's better. This 'betterness' manifests itself in better picture quality, stereo soundtrack and general overall quality. Like VHS above, and VHS-C (next entry), these cameras originated prior to the digital revolution and as such some of the older versions may cause a few problems when it comes time to edit on a computer – see later.

Plusses:

- Still held in high regard and widely used by the media and audio visual departments of various educational establishments.
- Its quality, while not being professional/industry standard, is still rather respectable.
- It possesses many, if not all, of the above mentioned features.
- It is large in size and, like the VHS, should give steady shots when filming off the tripod.
- They are usually very cheap to hire from community hire outlets.

Minuses:

- Although good, it still is not broadcast quality.
- The tapes are the same size as ordinary VHS tapes, making them cumbersome to carry around.
- The S-VHS tapes are not the cheapest video tape format to buy.

VHS-C

This is another member of the VHS clan. I first used one on a no-budget film a few years ago and was really taken aback by its relatively high quality, considering its small size. Being small, it has all the mobility advantages conferred by small cameras, although because VHS-C tapes aren't very big, this means they're only available in 30 or 45 minutes' duration. However, VHS-C tapes have adaptors, which means you can play the tapes on your video recorder after a hard day's filming, which is very convenient. It's a fine little camera, with a moderate price tag.

Plusses:

- Can be obtained quite cheaply. Now we are moving into the digital age, these cameras are coming down in price as people head to buy the new technology.
- Reasonable quality but, once again, not broadcast standard.
- The small compact tapes are easy to carry when you are out filming.
- The tape adaptors mean you can play back what you have just filmed on a normal video player.
- Many contain several of the aforementioned camera features.

Minuses:

- The fact that the tapes are only 30 or 45 minutes long can be a handicap to some film makers. You may run out of tape rather quickly while trying to get the take you want.
- Once again, this isn't a broadcast quality format.

Betacam

This is a broadcast camera and, up until several years ago, it was the standard camera used for anything from news stories to sit-coms to your favourite soap opera. It is quite big and hefty and can be placed on a tripod or shoulder. It uses a Beta cassette which lasts 30 minutes.

These types of cameras are available to rent from either corporate video studios (expensive), community camera rental services (cheaper, but still a tad hefty), or the local college (possibly free). The price difference in renting Betacam cameras from corporate or community organizations can literally be hundreds of pounds/dollars, not forgetting that you may be able to arrange something with a local college if they have any.

In short, it has good broadcast quality and you don't need a degree in electronics to use one. It is the little brother of the more high-tech/better quality and more prolific Digital Betacam.

Plusses:

- A broadcast quality (that is, television quality) camera – the benchmark that many first-timers head for.
- Has all the camera features, and a few more, mentioned on pages 32–33.
- It is relatively straightforward to master the basics.

- It is used by many companies and educational organizations, so plenty of places to obtain them from.
- It looks like a 'proper' camera – no one will mistake it for a home video.

Minuses:

- The tapes only last for around 30 minutes and this can cause problems if you are planing to do lots of filming.
- The tapes are expensive to buy.
- The tapes are bulky.
- You won't be able to play back what you have filmed unless you have access to a Beta player. It's not a case of taking an aerial lead from the camera to the nearest television to see what you have filmed.
- Don't think of buying one as the price tags are in the thousands.
- It is not the most mobile of cameras to carry around for great lengths of time.

Digital video cameras

The mid-90s saw the emergence of an important trend in film making and camera technology; things became digital and since this time the march of this technology has been irresistible and made its way into every avenue of film and television making.

In real terms, what has this meant for the film maker?

What this means is that the quality of cameras has increased; they are becoming cheaper and consequently more accessible. In basic technological terms they have become better and more capable than anything preceding them.

Also they are very much the norm. That's it in a nutshell!

Digital8 cameras

This camera format stems from the same tree as the Video8 camera and it, as the name suggests, is its digital counterpart. The Digital8 camera can be quite a compact and lightweight camera and therefore ease to carry around all day. It shares a lot of features and has a generically similar look and feel to the older model. It is a very common and reasonably priced piece of consumer technology.

Plusses:

- Good quality of image.
- A reasonably affordable camera.
- Compatible and ready for use with most computers for the purposes of digitizing your images and editing (see later).
- If you have the older (analog) Video8 format tapes then some Digital8 cameras can be used to play and digitize your footage onto a computer.
- A good 'entry-level' camera.

Minuses:

- Not a pro (professional) format – this is only a consumer-level camera remember, as such it is not used in the TV and film industry.
- Can be quite limited with regards to the features mentioned on pages 32 and 33.

MiniDV cameras

MiniDV cameras are perhaps the most popular consumer camera on the high street today. They combine high-tech gadgetry with ease of use; some require that you only switch them on, while others are more 'pro' orientated and have more features accordingly.

Some MiniDV formats are so good that they actually have the capability to record in DVCAM mode (see below).

They're small, light, becoming more numerous than rabbits in a field and offer near broadcast (television) or actual broadcast quality images. Between you and me, they're used a lot on satellite telelvision for outdoor reports and short films as well as being utilized, in part, for some documentary films.

They most popularly turn up in documentaries where people are sent off in survival situations and are given a camera to document their struggles, or in documentaries that follow people around in their daily lives. They also often serve the purpose of a 'back-up' or second camera in many fact-based programmes.

Plusses:

- Very high quality (but see minuses below).
- Very lightweight and mobile.
- The DVCAM record capability of some of them means you can get *even* better quality images.
- As the marketplace becomes more saturated and other formats come out (see HD below), the prices of some of these

cameras are coming down by a significant margin.

- Since a lot of computerized editing technology is geared up to MiniDV it is a convenient and good format to film on.
- The tapes used are small.
- The tapes last for over 60 minutes, so you can fit a lot onto them.
- They can be rented for reasonable rates.
- The are easy to use – you can learn the fundamental pointers in half an hour.
- They may have all the features you could possibly need.
- Unlike the previous two cameras, you may chance upon one of these for a few hundred pounds in the small ads.
- A technological 'mid-point', so to speak, between regular camcorders and professional systems. Combines ease of use with high quality.

Minuses:

- Although used extensively in television and some news reports, in strict terms they are not *really* broadcast quality cameras. Their real role is to supplement a full camera crew in access documentaries (following people around all the time) where turning up with a larger camera may be impractical, for example, when filming from the back seat of a police car and then running out as they chase some criminals. They are extremely good quality *but* you won't see an entire drama or TV film series made on one just yet.
- Although widely available they are expensive.

> When looking at digital cameras, try and find 3CCD (three chip) written on it as this indicates it's television quality.

DVCAM Cameras

These are a step up from the popular MiniDV format and are a popular professional format. They are very popular with television programme makers, many low-budget film makers, rock video directors and anyone else who manages to get their hands on them. They can be quite impressive cameras to look at as there is no mistaking that they are indeed a 'pro' format (they are big) and you can gain great kudos by carrying one around and then filming with it resting on your shoulder.

They are relatively easy to use – you don't need to be a genius to competently use one.

Plusses:

- If you can't get hold of any DVCAM tapes you can sometimes use MiniDV tapes – many DVCAM cameras are compatible with the smaller format.
- Some DV tapes are very, very long and you can fit over three hours of footage on one – now that's long!
- Can still be a relatively lightweight format that means you don't need a fork-lift truck to carry it around.
- Most computerized editing technology is geared up to this format.
- This is a broadcast quality camera format – this benchmark is the 'grail' of many low-budget film makers.

Minuses:

- This format is very expensive to buy (pro format, remember), although they can be hired for reasonable rates.
- Although tapes aren't that expensive, they are still more expensive than what you will be used to (and feel like paying).
- These cameras tend to have black and white viewfinders and no flip-out screens. If you're used to camcorders with these features, then DV cameras will take a bit of getting used to.

HDD cameras

These cameras are Hard Disk Drive cameras (hence the initials) and, as the name suggests, they carry no recording tape, but instead have a small internal drive. As such there is no need to carry tapes around with you when you go out filming.

In terms of price and handling they can be quite affordable and some can be incredibly compact. However, as this is very much a consumer product, they can be rather on the basic side in terms of the features and functions they have. Like some other formats mentioned in this chapter, HDD isn't a pro format.

Plusses:

- Decent picture quality.
- Small size – easy to carry around or put in your coat pocket.
- No pesky tapes to carry around during a long day's filming.
- Can film, and store, a fair amount depending on the capacity of the disk.

Minuses:

- If you run out of memory during your filming, you may have to delete things in order to carry on filming.

- Quite a basic camera – may not be able to do 'intricate' filming due to its limited features.
- Once again, this isn't a pro format.

HD (High Definition) and HDV cameras

These relatively new arrivals on the film-making scene are the next 'groundswell' in camera technology. In simple terms they are one up from digital cameras (many even take the same tapes) and have made rapid in-roads to television production and many feature films. In terms of what they offer the film maker, these cameras produce a high quality image that is clear and sharp.

HD is the professional end of the range that is used within in the broadcast and film industry, while HDV is the consumer equivalent. They share lots in common with any other video-based format out there and if you know your way around one camera, an HD camera should hold no surprises for you. Some HD cameras now have **solid state** recording which means they don't need tapes – this can have some serious benefits when it comes to the editing process (see later).

Just like many of the other formats described elsewhere in this chapter, the HD family has its own spectrum, i.e. there are the smaller compact ones and the rather big ones used to shoot feature films. So, just because you buy into this type of camera does not automatically guarantee that you'll be producing material of the same standard as what Hollywood has to offer.

Plusses:

- Quite simple to use.
- Some can use the same tapes as a digital camera.
- High quality of filmed image.
- Some modern edit systems already have HD-compatible edit software ready to handle this format (however, see Minuses below).

Minuses:

- The consumer end of the range can be a bit limited with regards to the features mentioned on pages 32 and 33.
- The cameras at the top end of the range versions are very expensive to buy; the pro formats cost thousands and thousands.
- Relatively expensive to hire.
- As HD footage is of a superior quality, not all edit systems will be able to handle the footage – it has to be HD enabled.

DVD Camcorders

It finally happened! They've made a video camera where you record onto a DVD! Well, this was inevitable, wasn't it? So what do these cameras bring to the low-budget/first-time film maker?

These cameras fit in very snugly with all the other modern consumer media products that are out there and you should have no trouble plugging it into PCs, laptops etc. for editing and viewing; they are all part of the same big electronic family.

As a camera their performance is pretty adequate and more or less on a par with some of the other cameras that use tapes. Now, one between-the-lines thing to consider about this camera is no-one I know who works in TV or film has ever used one in a professional context. Without totally shooting this format down in flames, I think it's worth bearing in mind that these DVD cameras, despite their popularity, have yet to mature into a recognized and serious format.

However, watch this space...

Plusses:

- Records onto DVD – can make it a cheap format to film with!
- Compatible with most PCs and other consumer audio-visual equipment.
- If you are editing on a PC you can upload the images straight into an editing package (see later).

Minuses:

- They can be expensive.
- They can have quite basic recording features.

'The Others'...

What are 'The Others'?

These are things like digital stills cameras, phones and other devices that now have some limited video recording capability.

Although these are not designed primarily as video recording devices it is worth giving them a mention as they have permeated into our technological culture to an extent where people now use them instead of a 'proper' video camera. How many times have you seen someone holding their mobile phone at arm's length to film or take a photo of something (maybe you do it yourself)? Needless to say there is quite a gap in quality between a decent digital stills camera with video recording feature and a mobile/cell phone. Even then, a stills camera may be seriously limited in terms of functions and memory – there is no way you should think about filming anything over a couple of minutes on one as you'll have to keep downloading your footage all the time – the same goes for a phone.

So why use them?

Well, increasingly today we are seeing news stories that feature footage shot on these video devices by members of the public, as well as field reporters talking to us live through the grainy and blurred pictures of a video phone. Likewise, many mainstream film makers have been quick to pick up on this. You may see a film that features footage shot on a video phone of some mocked-up disaster or news event. When an audience sees this it looks real as they are so used to seeing images of this quality associated with certain television news reports.

Worth thinking about for your film perhaps?

Film cameras

If you don't like video, then how about entering the world of film? But remember, film doesn't record sound. Although, so saying, some film does have magnetic strips on the side for recording sound. More importantly, it's an expensive medium and you can't 'record' over film. Once it has been exposed, that's it, no second go. Also, you will have to consider the various types of films that are available. Some film types achieve certain looks and 'feels' to them and are suited to specific light conditions.

'Plusses' and 'minuses' are given only after the first film camera format, so as not to be repetitive, because all the fundamental points are the same for the remaining formats. Remember that when you are thinking about using film it is always a case of the balance between the cost and complexity of using it versus the fact it's *film*, the format every first-time film maker would like to use if only they could.

Super 8 mm

The 'camcorder' of many a year ago, this little camera now lives in yard sales, the backs of garages and specialist film shops. It pops its head up from time to time in various pop videos –

usually the flickering moody bits on tour buses or backstage. It is also used in low-budget films as well as in some television adverts. This camera is small, hand-held and, if sprayed silver, can double as a gun in your sci-fi film.

Usually battery powered or with a wind-up mechanism, these cameras, depending on make and model, may include some basic filming indicators in the viewfinder, although they are nowhere near as comprehensive and helpful as the ones you will find on a video camera. The best example of this is if you were to film in a dark room. Since a Super 8 camera uses an optical view finder (just glass and lenses) you may think it looks OK to film, but if you were to do the same with any camcorder you would immediately see, and know, that the image in the viewfinder was dark. Also, there's no way to play back what you've just filmed until it's developed and put through a projector – just like all other film formats!

Although it gives a very rustic and arty film look, it can be a nightmare to use. Not only is film a very 'unforgiving' format for sourcing images, it's also very expensive – a standard Super 8mm film of a mere 2^1/$_2$ minutes will cost the same as four one-hour MiniDV tapes. This means you can waste considerable sums of money trying to get things right. However, you can pick up the cameras for next to nothing in the back of old curio shops, which can make them cheap to buy. They can literally be picked up for the same price as a few bottles of beer.

Plusses:

- You can obtain these cameras for very little money.
- They are simple to use (see Minuses below).
- They can last for ages.
- They are highly mobile.
- It is the cheapest film format to buy and use.
- The film can be obtained from most decent photographic shops.
- It is film!

Minuses:

- Although simple to use there is no immediate way of knowing if what you are filming will come out well.
- Although the film is 'cheap', it doesn't last very long.
- You will need a special 8 mm film splicer/editor to piece things together. Or you could get it transferred direct onto a tape format (see Chapter 12), but this is expensive.

- It doesn't normally record sound.
- You can't plug this format into the back of your television.
- You have to wait for your film to be developed to see it.
- The cameras can be very noisy which can interfere with your sound recording.

16 mm and Super 16 mm

These film camera formats are still steady stalwarts of television, adverts, pop videos and many feature films. It was the format used to film the cult movie *This is Spinal Tap*, as well as the low-budget hit *Clerks*. Most people are exposed to this format while watching major television drama films.

Put in crude and simple terms, *regular* 16 mm looks a tad grainy, while Super 16 mm looks glossy and lighter. To give a visual reference, many famous and 'cheesy' 1970s crime and cop television series were filmed on *regular* 16 mm.

To get hold of one you might have to call around a few places. You could try asking your local photographic supplier, or some community camera centres may even house one or know where one can be acquired along with the film. Like 8 mm, they can be found in attic sales etc. Since, like all film cameras, they're primarily a mechanical device, they can last for ages. The last 16 mm shoot I went on for part of an American television documentary used a 16 mm camera from the 1950s.

Like all film camera systems, 16 mm is nowhere near as easy (or as cheap) as video formats. You will have lots and lots of things to get right (especially the light) if you are to film something that doesn't turn out as just dark blurred images.

35 mm

Whenever you go to the cinema, it is likely that you are watching 35 mm film. It's the standard mainstream film format. As such, you should be able to think of many examples and recall the kind of look and feel it can give.

However, it's incredibly expensive, and that's just the film. To give you a very rough idea of the cost of using 35 mm film, read on. The film used in most photographic cameras is also 35 mm. It's expensive, isn't it? At the time of writing it will cost you hundreds to buy a 400 ft reel of 35 mm film. At normal speed (not slow motion, for example) this will last six minutes. When you film, it will always take a while before you get things right – this is otherwise know as the **shooting ratio** – the number of minutes you actually film set against the number of minutes that make it into the film. Sometimes the ratio can be very high. On top of the cost of purchasing of the film, it also has to be developed and printed; the cost of this is likewise respectively high. Then there are the negative costs to think about, which you will need further copies to be made.

Now for the camera itself. A brand new top of the range camera can literally cost more than a house.

This can all get very, very expensive. You may soon be confronted with a colossal figure.

However, these are not the only kinds of camera that exist. There are Umatic, Hi-8, as well as cutting-edge digital formats that are being used in big-budget motion pictures. To list every format, with related variants, would be very confusing, so try out a few formats yourself, decide on what you want, and stick to it – otherwise you may get lost in a never-ending world of camera technology.

There are some people who like to mix and merge formats when making a film. Perhaps the most famous exponent of this is the director Oliver Stone. Check out his films *Natural Born Killers* and *JFK* to see how effective and dramatic swapping between formats can be. Some pop video directors do this quite frequently as well and call the genre 'anti-video'. A more recent example of this is *The Blair Witch Project*, which swapped between a camcorder and black and white 16 mm film.

From my own experience of making films, speaking to other film makers and going to low-budget film meetings, I have found that it is Betacam, DVCAM, MiniDV and HDV cameras that come in equal first place (with 16 mm coming a very distant second). The reasons being that they are simple to use, relatively cheap to rent, give superb quality and you can record over what you've filmed. All things that don't fit into the equation when using film cameras.

Choosing the type of camera to use on your first film is a perfect example of a trade-off. You will have to consider what you ideally want and then rationalize this with what is possible. The most common trade-off in the world of low-budget film making is people wanting to make their first film on the format of film, and when that becomes impossible they move back to the next best thing which is obtaining a broadcast quality system, and if that is not possible seeing what else they can get hold of. I would say that obtaining broadcast quality cameras is the most common trade-off situation.

If I had not accepted this trade-off when I was making my first film, then I would probably still be trying to make it even now! But remember, no matter how good or 'street cred' a camera system is, it doesn't compose the shots and make your film interesting. It is up to the director to take any camera and use his or her vision to create interesting pictures. Robert Rodriguez (*Desperado, Dusk Till Dawn* and *Spy Kids*) made his first films with a VHS camera.

Conversely, some years ago a couple of low-budget film makers managed a bit of a coup and were able to make a short film on 35 mm for the purposes of impressing some television and film bigwigs. The logic they had at the screening was, 'This is 35 mm film, we are great'. Unfortunately, the film was rather flat and failed to impress anyone at the screening despite their pleas that, 'This is 35 mm, it has got to be great!' They were trading on the format they used instead of what they did with it. So, having an amazing format does not automatically translate into making great pictures.

Everyone would love to make their feature debut on film (35 mm ideally), but the factors of complexity, cost, developing, availability and sheer hassle dictate otherwise. However, as with many things in the process of making a film, don't let those obstacles block your way. Depending on how much energy, tenacity and determination you have, you may just find a way of getting hold of the camera that you have your heart set on. The world of film making is full of people going through absolute agony and degradation in their quest and dream to get their story made. Treat it like a fanatical desire, otherwise you may not do all you want to. The choice is yours – although it's worth bearing in mind that many first timers make an 'advert' on a broadcast system and then show it in the hope of having their idea made into a fully fledged feature movie with film.

Closing thoughts on camera technology

Every few years there is a new camera format that comes out and dazzles everyone with its charms and abilities. In their droves, TV and film people rush out to buy into this new format while cruelly throwing away the cameras they were using yesterday. I call this 'The Emperor's New Clothes syndrome' and what I mean is that some of the discarded camera formats are perfect, there was nothing wrong with them – only their age. Likewise, people are rushing towards the newer format simply because it happens to be the latest thing.

Due to this trend there are various capable and good camera formats that are now ignored and unused simply because they fell out of fashion. As a first-time/low-budget film maker it's up to you to steer clear of this entrapment and decide what format is best for you and your film. Do not be swayed by technology.

Did you know?

Did you ever wonder where the word *footage* comes from when talking about what you have filmed? When you buy movie film you don't say, 'I'll have one hour's worth', you say 'I'll have 400 hundred foot worth' – film is measured in feet. There you go!

Bottom-line rules of cameras

- Give serious thought to using a video system as they're way easier to use than film.
- Don't get hung up on the fact that you haven't got a state of the art or professional system. So long as your camera records moving images, that is all that matters.
- Because digital cameras are rising in popularity, older style formats are becoming cheaper.
- I don't want to discourage anyone from using a format they really have their heart set on, but remember that film is a tricky format to get your head around if you are not experienced.

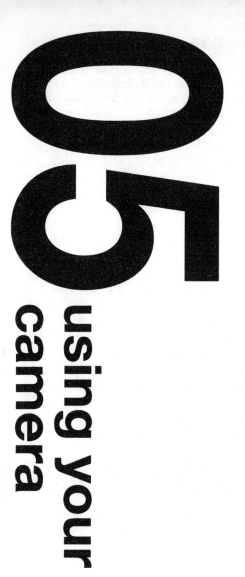

05 using your camera

In this chapter you will learn:
- how to look after your camera
- some basic and effective camera techniques
- fantastic and easy film tricks and 'cheats'.

Anyone know how to use this thing?

A script, camera and people are the essential components of making a film; look on anything else you manage to get hold of as a bonus. Therefore, it is imperative that you learn how to use the camera you have chosen to the limit of its ability. The reason for this is that technical details, such as camera operation, can be learned – it is an objective quantity. However, creativity, which of course you already have, is something you cannot learn. You either have it or you don't.

Making a film is about combining creativity and technology, so it is vitally important that you learn to use your camera. Being able to combine your creativity with the know-how to use a certain camera format will make you very formidable when you are creating your film.

If you don't know how to use a camera, you will find yourself severely limited when the time comes to start filming. You may have to rely on someone who may not be creative and is more interested in the latest technology. Also, you may find it incredibly difficult and frustrating trying to communicate your vision of how to film a certain scene or shot to the operator. Some people just view a camera as a neat bit of kit, others see it as something to help make something entertaining and enjoyable to look at.

Where to find help

If you don't know how to use any of the camera systems mentioned, there are many ways in which you can find out about them.

If your ambitions lie along film camera lines then have a look for amateur film societies in your local library or *Yellow Pages* to see where the nearest one is. I think these places are great as the last bastions of small-scale cine-film know-how in today's video age. They usually hold meetings, workshops and screenings of what the club's members have made.

You may find that some of these groups are very eager to help you, allowing for free time, how persuasive you are and if they like your idea. One advantage with these groups is the obvious fact that they will own, and maybe hire out, the type of format you are looking for, or maybe know where there is an old 16 mm camera lying around. If you stumble across such a group you will not only have found a decent bunch of film enthusiasts, but also an entire support network that may be able to work wonders and help you out with your project. Remember, film isn't a cheap thing to use, and editing it is another headache, so these groups may collectively have all the tools you need to get things going. Although they may look like middle-aged ramblers or folk singers (as I have found) you may discover they have been responsible for some rather bizarre films in the past – but that's film makers for you! Such people should serve to highlight that there is a lot of integrity among film makers. They can be blissfully unselfish with regards to helping out an aspiring John Huston.

If there is no such society in your area, then there will be a university or college somewhere that undertakes courses in film making – maybe up to 16 mm format. I don't mean that you have to *enrol* on these courses, merely approach the department and explain what you are hoping to do. You'll quite likely get some interested 'alternative' types showing an interest.

Just as steam ships overtook sail, the same is true of video and film. There will be infinitely more places that deal in the teaching, hiring and generally specializing in video cameras than film. Most colleges and higher education establishments will have courses dealing in the operation of professional broadcast cameras. Your *Yellow Pages* will list at least five companies that make corporate videos (i.e. for business or training films), or maybe wedding videos, on Betacam or digital systems. Basically they've taken over, leaving film as a very specialized, perhaps antiquated 'plaything'. I'll put it this way: when was the last time you saw a cheesy advert for your local car lot on flickering film reels being projected at your local cinema? A sub-plot of the film *Boogie Nights* is largely about the change from film to video.

I couldn't possibly explain how to operate all of the camera systems here as, apart from taking up the rest of this book, you need to learn in a 'hands-on' way. Also, your local library will stock books that will tell you the ins and outs of the more commercially available video systems (visit the photography section).

Looking after your camera

Once you have found somewhere to learn about and get your hands on your chosen system, there are a few things that you should get into the habit of doing.

Theft

An important rule to remember is to keep an eye on your kit at all times. It's not surprising that cameras and the associated paraphernalia attract a lot of attention from passers-by and those in the area. Not all of this attention is favourable. There has been many a film crew out at night filming a documentary who have turned around to find that the tripod is missing or there's no camera. Owing to the legal and bureaucratic nature of television and film companies today, there's usually some form that has to be filled in before a crew can go out. One of the risks on these forms includes 'theft' – it's a major threat in cities and other places.

I know of one tale of woe concerning a film crew who were making a gritty film about life on unemployment benefit and poor housing on a notorious British housing project. The director thought he knew it all and disregarded the warnings of the local fixer (person who sets up and arranges things) by retorting, 'Don't bother me. I've been to Beirut, I've been shot!' As the crew were introducing themselves to the owners of a property, the van they had come in was broken into and all their gear was stolen. All this happened in the space of one minute from a distance of about 50 feet.

Transporting your camera

Use the carry case that comes with the camera. If your camera didn't come with such an accessory then try to improvise one from something. I don't need to tell you that a camera is one of the most important things when making a film – look after it. It's often tempting to carry the camera clutched in one hand as you go from place to place, or have it slung around your neck like some obscene medallion. Such treatment will shorten the life of your camera. Remember that modern cameras are made up of largely fragile and precisely made components, and jolts, bumps and drops can stop them from working. A professional film crew has quite a few bright silver flight cases full of gear when out on location; it is a chore for them, but every day before filming the cameras are taken out carefully and, after a long day's work, they are put back in again. Camera operators going on location often moan about the amount of gear they've got to put in boxes and carry around, but it's the only way of transporting these things safely.

Beware of the elements

Protecting your camera against the elements is another thing to consider if you are planning on filming outside. Cameras do not like water, especially video cameras. All it takes is one drop of water to ruin things and effectively scupper your plans. The best way to avoid this is simply not to go filming when it starts to rain. However, there may be times when this is not an option and you will have to obtain some kind of protection. Since professional camera rain and water protection 'jackets' cost a fortune, and they don't exist for domestic cameras, the tried and tested method is to use a decent quality and sturdy plastic bag. Although crude and a bit messy to use, it is very effective. Just place an appropriate-sized plastic bag over the camera 'poncho style', then cut holes for the lens and viewfinder (taking into account the variable positions of the viewfinder), using masking tape to seal and waterproof the joins. I once used this method while filming a car rally one rainy day, wedged between ITV and BBC news camera crews, and although my water proofing method looked embarrassing in such prestigious company, it did the job brilliantly. The drawback with this method is that it can be rather fiddly when it's time to change the tapes. This is a procedure best done inside, as the pervading dampness in the air can get into your camera and jam the mechanism for a while. Avoid rain, is the lesson here – even the slightest hazy drizzle can build up on your camera's plastic exterior and turn into a mini torrent that invariably makes a beeline straight for the master electronic circuits.

Still on the same subject, one way that rain conspires to ruin filming is to leave droplets on the lens. In the madness of filming, these tiny conspirators are very hard to notice. Although the larger of them can be seen and carefully wiped off the lens with an appropriate material (not the cuff of a duffel coat!), their smaller brethren are invisible both on the lens and in the viewfinder. Therefore, when you look back at what you have filmed on a television, there will be a drop awkwardly covering the left eye of your lead actor or hanging mysteriously in the air above your actors like a surreal spacecraft. They really can spoil things. This is one of the reasons why people use monitors (see later). To guard against rain droplets getting on the lens while filming, it is advisable to use a hood (although rain is not a hood's only reason for existence). A hood fits around the lens and extends outwards a short distance like a mini tunnel, offering limited protection from the rain, without lessening the field of vision. Some of the more modern domestic cameras have one fitted, though they are rarely big enough to be totally effective, and older cameras won't have this feature at all. A good way to make a better one is to take four square pieces of plastic (CD box covers, for example) and gaffer tape them around your lens in a box arrangement, DIY-style, making sure they don't get into shot. This will lessen (but not remove) your chances of getting rain on the lens – but try to film facing away from the wind!

Another environmental problem is when you are filming somewhere cold and damp and condensation forms on the lens. This is easy to remove, with a careful wipe of the lens or by letting the lens 'breathe' for a few moments. The only reason I mention this is because it formed on my camera lens when I was filming a restaurant scene in a half-derelict cellar and I thought the camera was suffering a major fault.

Finally, bright sunlight. Although the friend of all film makers (see the section on well-lit scenes, later), I have known a few small cameras to literally be cooked and effectively destroyed by the heat of the sun. Many cameras are black, or dark coloured, and this is a disadvantage when it is very sunny as the camera will become progressively hotter. It is not unheard of for the heat to reach levels where it has buckled and warped a spooling mechanism, melted a tape or simply 'fried' some circuit. So once again, cover your camera with a suitable material (e.g. a white cloth) if you consider the weather too hot.

Basic filming techniques

Using a tripod

When using a small camcorder, you can attach it to the end of a tripod, as per usual, and create quite an interesting film 'tool'. I discovered this trick by sheer accident one day, and found that this set-up allows you to use the camera as a sort of lasso – you can just swing it around the place when you are filming things. For example, you can fix the tripod to its maximum extension and then hold it by the 'feet', which allows you to have the camera a considerable distance above your head (see Figure 2). With this you could film over a tall wall, in the branches of a tree, or you could just spin it around, depending on what you wanted to do. It's like having an 'eye' on the top of a pole.

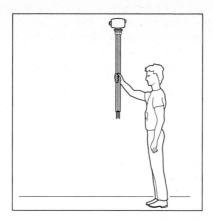

figure 2

You can manipulate it, twist it and swing it around to get an incredible range of views and shots that would otherwise require some very specialist and expensive equipment. Even then it would be rather slow moving compared with this method. You can also suddenly and dramatically increase the height of the shot, by holding on to the base of the tripod and shoving it into the air – making sure that the camera is pointing at your subject, of course. For example, you could have a shot of a man walking down the street and raise the height of the camera as he's moving along (see Figures 3 and 4). Such a sudden moveshot would be very powerful and would give your film a really strong style (more of this later). Using this method you could also film a fast, frenetic party by swinging, increasing height, shoving in between people and so on. This method can add a new dimension to your films.

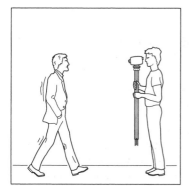

figure 3

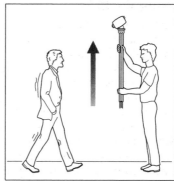

figure 4

Video cameras that have flip-out view screens really come into their own with these techniques as you don't have to rely on the viewfinder to see what you are filming. Perhaps you can think of some other moves using this method.

Not only is there the energetic shot element to this 'camera rig', but it has the advantage of being a steadier way of filming. When you hold the camcorder in both hands and clutch it close to your chest, every step and move you make will result in a very shaky and bumpy picture. Using this 'lasso' method, you create a much more fluid picture. For example, say you are using the camcorder to film someone from the side as they walk down the street. If you were holding the camera close to your chest and squinting intensely into the viewfinder, not only would the shot be rather bumpy, but you would also risk falling over or walking into a lamp post. With the camera on the tripod, you can hold it by the 'neck' and just point the camera at the subject while alternating between looking at what you are filming and where you are going.

The shot will tend to be steadier as your elbow acts as a kind of 'damper', with the tripod legs acting as a 'counter-weight', so reducing the shake. With some practice you will soon learn what your camera's **field of vision** is and improve your method for keeping things steady.

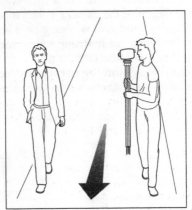

figure 5

Warning: Do not attempt the above method with a larger camera as it will be very heavy and nigh-on impossible to manipulate. In some instances the camera might come off the tripod and spoil your directorial aspirations with a loud shattering crash!

Using coloured filters

Another tip to make your camerawork more interesting is to use coloured filters – easily obtainable from your nearest quality photographic shop.

Using filters adds a sometimes surreal or moody effect to a shot. For example, imagine if you were in a disused quarry and you were to hold a piece of red coloured glass in front of your eyes – instant alien planet. Or if you were in a wood and did the same with dark blue glass – night-time effect just like a Hammer Horror film.

Not all filters are one uniform colour across the glass; some are graduated. These filters have a coloured strip at the top that fades in colour down the glass. So if you were to film something with it, such as a landscape shot of a field for example, the sky would be tinged with a certain colour, while the ground would be normal, leaving the buildings or actors you were filming untouched. Have a look at any Jerry Bruckheimer-produced blockbusters (*The Rock, Con Air, Gone in 60 Seconds, Black Hawk Down*) to see how cool and delicious graduated filters can be when used in some shots. There is actually a quarry I know of that, with the use of filters, has been used for several different alien planets (for the same television series) as well as a Roman gladiatorial arena.

Tricks with film

Since 8 mm film can be a fiddly thing to use, there is a way to roughly simulate it, using even the cheapest of video cameras. If your camera has a manual gain control (see page 33), this will make the picture rather grainy. When a grainy and fuzzy picture is made black and white it looks quite similar to black and white 8 mm film. Very street cred and very arty.

To give a shot a bit of *bite*, try out something known as the 'Dutch **Tilt**'. This is a very simple and effective camera technique achieved by using a tripod with one leg shorter than the rest – or by just resting it on the ground and tilting it. This has the effect of making everything seem to be at an angle (the steepness will depend on how you have set up the camera). This can make things look creepy, disturbing, unnatural and downright funky. It is also a good way of exaggerating the height of something. If you have a tilt looking upwards at a building, or even a person, the effect will be near giddying. Simple and effective. Try it out.

Still keeping with tilting cameras, a clever and funny way to simulate someone climbing up a steep cliff, or the outside of a building, is to place your camera on its side on an appropriate surface. This will make the ground appear as a vertical surface, and you can then have your actors stooping forwards, pulling themselves 'up' on a rope. Anyone who has watched the 1960s series of Batman will have seen this in most episodes. Be careful, however, not to arrange the shot so that trees are growing horizontally out of the 'mountain'.

If you want to create the impression that someone in your film is being watched or stalked, film through some bushes or tree leaves. This will automatically feel as if someone is hiding and spying on a character.

Finally there comes one of my favourite tricks: move in, **zoom out**. You may have witnessed this slightly unsettling effect in a few films, but one of the most famous examples is in *Jaws*, when Roy Scheider's character is on the beach and there are shouts of 'Shark' from the water. The camera rushes up to him, but it appears as though the background is expanding.

This effect is achieved by moving the camera directly towards your actor, while at the same time zooming out with your camera. It's an effect that even the cheapest camcorder can manage. It takes a bit of practice and helps if the move towards the actor is smooth and in a straight line, and the speed of the zoom out equals the move of the camera. Simple and free.

Get to know your camera, experiment with it and make sure it works hard for you!

Bottom-line rules of using cameras

- Remember the anecdote about the 35 mm film flop from the previous chapter? It's not the format that tells the story, it is the person behind the camera. A creative person can make a 'bad' camera take great pictures that tell a superb story; a 'great' camera, on its own, is just an inert piece of machinery.

- Get to know your camera inside out so that you can achieve the best results from it.

- Respect and look after your camera at all times – without it you have no film!

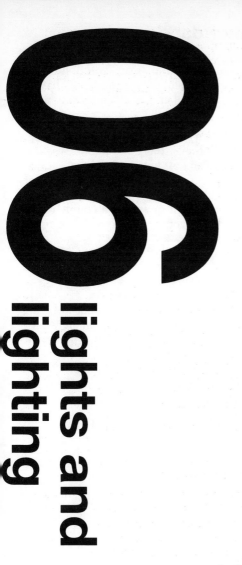

06

lights and lighting

In this chapter you will learn:
- about the different types of lights available
- how to achieve superb lighting effects with minimum resources
- a few basic safety tips for you, your cast and crew.

This room's rather dark!

Not only will you need a camera to film your masterpiece, but you will also need some kind of illumination. You don't need huge lighting rigs and its quite possible that you already have a suitable light in your house that will effectively illuminate what you are filming.

Depending on the light sensitivity of the camera you are using, and the mood you want to achieve, there are lots of ways to improvise. I would suggest starting off with as much light on set as possible and then, if required, work your way down. For example, if you have bright lights that are blinding everyone, all you need to do is turn them around or switch a couple off to obtain the desired effect. However, trying to squeeze more power out of a candle is impossible.

Lighting your set

Most camcorders and smaller film cameras have built-in lights, or slots for external lights, that you can use to illuminate what's directly in front of the camera. However, if the light is built in, it will drain your camera battery much more quickly than normal. It can also give the game away because the light will be shining merrily away on everything the camera is pointing at. Thus the audience will think, 'They've got a light on that camera.'

There is a flip side to this, however: a camera light does have an 'artistic' use as it's a good way of simulating someone's view as they walk slowly through a dark and deserted building at night, for example, with the light acting as a torch on a hard hat. Give it a go.

Bedside and household lights can be very useful (they worked for Robert Rodriguez) and you can change their brightness by fitting them with different wattage bulbs. Do check the maximum wattage information, which should be somewhere on the appliance, as some bedside lights aren't always happy with a high-wattage bulb and you could end up with an unanticipated 'special effect'! Alternatively, you might find that normal wall or ceiling lights work perfectly well.

Experiment using different coloured light bulbs which can drastically alter moods (just as filters can outdoors). A red light can make things either erotic or evil, and a blue one will create a cold and haunting atmosphere. Also, 500-watt halogen lights are very good for lighting up somewhere outdoors in the middle of the night – although there isn't always an available plug socket in the thick of a forest.

> **Warning!**
> 500-watt halogen (and higher wattage) lights get very hot, so if you want to adjust the angle of the light use a pair of pliers or a pair of 'asbestos gloves'.

These powerful lights not only present handling problems, they can also make it very uncomfortable for the people on set. Seeing sweat pour down someone's face can cause some unpleasant aesthetic problems in close-ups and, more importantly, people have a nasty tendency to faint under such lighting. You would be surprised how many camera people pass out every week in television and film studios.

In addition, 500-watt halogen lights are very bright, so if you are in a small room filming an intimate romantic scene, the presence of such a powerful light might suggest to the audience that a hydrogen bomb has detonated nearby. Angling the light beam can correct this, but it would be better to use a more appropriate light. These 500-watt lights are also known as garden lights. They are inexpensive and widely available at your nearest home shop or lighting specialist.

If you want to have a look at what the professionals use, then ask for '**Redheads**' or lights made by 'Arri'. They have barn doors on them, metal doors that resemble flat rose petals, so that light coming from the bulb can be lessened or increased depending on their configuration. Coloured transparent paper called '**gels**' can be attached to these barn doors with bulldog clips to adjust the colour of the light. As with 500-watt lights, these barn doors get very hot, so be careful when handling them! Some community camera suppliers hire them out for about £15/US$20 a day. However, as with many things in film making, with particular reference to the above 'pro' lights, you can effectively improvise something else for much less money, or none at all.

Depending on the kind of lights you want, pay very close attention to its needs. For example, a 500-watt light will not use a standard 13 amp fuse found in the plug of your PlayStation. If you get things wrong you might plug it in and be met with a loud pop, a blue flash, a melted bulb, a blown fuse box and the irate comments of whoever owns or manages the building you are filming in. Try to get someone, preferably with a modicum of electrical know-how, to help you if you have your heart set on the more powerful lights.

Safety tip

If you end up with a set of powerful lights, think about investing in a circuit breaker. This will prevent you overloading and blowing up a humble domestic electric system as it will cut out before an accident happens.

Lighting effects

Lighting is something that all too often gets overlooked. First-time camera users have a tendency to start filming without having taken much stock of lighting requirements. If filming has taken place with low lighting levels then your footage will look hazy and grainy. It may also mean you experience focusing problems as you can't see what you are filming. Light is a vital ingredient to the film-making recipe and, just like any recipe, there are loads of ways to spice things up. Simple experimentation can produce some rather stunning effects. Even Martin Scorcese once admitted in a television interview that he 'didn't have a clue about lights'.

The lighting effect for a particular scene is up to you. Do you want long shadows? Do you want it bright or dark and dismal? As director it's your say and you make all the decisions. Here are a few money-saving and improvised lighting effects that may inspire you to think of and dream up some of your own:

- **Simulating a group of people watching television.** Have a bright blue light shining on your actors and then quickly wave a piece of paper in front of it to simulate the changing pictures of a television. The light from a real television is rarely bright enough for filming.
- **Making a fire without a matchbox or petrol tin.** Shine some powerful coloured lights, preferably orange, at a reflector (see below) and then wobble it as you bounce the light to your thespians. Obviously this is just a lighting effect and does not include sound and smoke!
- **Lightning outdoors.** Obtain aforementioned 500-watt lights, or something more powerful if possible, and then cover the light with a non-flammable material to make sure there is no 'light leakage'. Then, when you want lightning, uncover the

light and then cover again as per the desired duration. Covering and uncovering the light is much preferable to switching the power on and off as this risks blowing the bulb. However, beware that lightning is usually accompanied by rain – water and powerful lighting don't really mix very well... Also, light disperses rather quickly outdoors so your light will have to be relatively close to whatever you are filming to be effective.

- **Lightning 'indoors'.** Have the same set-up as above, but place the light as close to a window as possible, while still allowing someone to cover and uncover the light. The lightning will shine through the window and into the set/room you are filming in but, since it is indoors, you won't have to worry about creating 'rain'.

- **Someone looking into shimmering water.** Shine a bright light on to a sizeable piece of reflective material, such as cooking foil, which has been crumpled and therefore reflects the light very unevenly. Then angle the reflective material so that the light bounces up into the actor's face and move it around slowly and rhythmically. The result will be that the actor's face is 'painted' with sparkling and moving points of light. One thing to mention here is that this trick is only effective on sunny days (otherwise where would the reflected light come from?) but can cause a problem as the lighting you are using may get lost in the natural sunlight, so you will have to keep the lights and the reflector quite close to the actor's face. However, using this effect on a cloudy dull day would look very supernatural.

- **Car lights pulling into a driveway at night**. Make sure your lights are held in a safe and manageable way. Someone then stands in front of the window of a living room and swings the lights across the glass in one smooth motion, making sure they don't start and stop on the glass. When filming in the darkened room, it will appear as if car headlights have just gone through the room. Bear in mind, though, that if you are filming towards the window, you need to keep the the curtains closed, otherwise your car will be revealed for what it is – someone holding a light! The light in the room will also have to be at a suitable level for the 'car headlights' to be seen.

Using reflectors

Reflectors are another tool you probably know about. They are large pieces of reflective material that people hold as though they are about to catch an invisible pancake. They are used for boosting and redistributing light on a set without the need to move equipment about, and are best employed when filming outdoors in the absence of artificial light, so that you can reflect sunlight wherever you want. You won't always need them – and you might not need them at all – but like other things in film making, it can be effectively and cheaply improvised.

To make one you will need some lightweight material, such as cardboard, and then cover it with tin foil. The shiny side of the foil will make a hard reflector, and the duller side will act as a diffuse reflector.

Be mindful that reflectors can't bounce light over great distances and they have to be positioned rather close to the people or the things you are filming. Some of your shots may have to be framed (more later) rather tightly to avoid filming a hapless soul holding a reflector.

Basic positioning

Changing the position of your lights can alter the mood of your scene in a variety of ways:

- Placing a bright light under someone so that it points upwards will make that person's face very sinister and evil looking. You've probably all seen this, when someone has been outside at night shining a torch under their chin. I once used this simple torch method when making a documentary about a theatrical society's 'ghost walk' through a park at night. It gave some incredibly strong images. It's just one way in which a tweak of the lights can give a powerful effect.
- The opposite of placing the light under the subject is, of course, placing the light above the subject. This has a completely different effect, as it makes the person look rather angelic, as if surrounded by an aura of spiritual light. This effect has been used *loads* of times on the *X-Files*; practically every other episode there's a scene where Mulder and Scully are rushing through a forest at night and then suddenly see someone in the middle of a forest clearing. That person will usually be lit from above and it gives them a really surreal and unearthly quality. This effect is also used in dream scenes where someone appears in the middle of a black empty space, producing that ghostly look.
- Staying with this unearthly side of lighting, another popular and easy method to give your film a certain level of 'forteaness' is to boost the light levels up as much as you can.

To see examples of this type of lighting, check out most films where aliens walk out of their space craft. The lighting is usually all the way up to reinforce the 'divine-like' entrance of the creature. *Close Encounters of the Third Kind* used this method to superb effect. It was also utilized in *Poltergeist* in the scenes where ghosts started appearing. As the lady in that film says, 'Run into the light'.

However, when using the above method you should be aware of the iris feature on your camera. If you are using a camcorder with an auto-iris feature, then you probably won't be able to get the last effect as the camera will automatically down-adjust the light level to what *it* thinks is an acceptable level. (See what I mean on page 32 about trying to get a camera with a *manual* iris control?) What you are essentially trying to do here is **overexpose** your footage.

- Side-lighting is another basic way of altering the mood of a shot. As the name suggests, a light is placed to the side of an actor and lights up only one side of the face. This is used a lot, especially on baddies in the corner of a darkened room, to emphasize their 'shady' side, or some other criminal/deranged type sitting at a table about to describe how they are going to torture the hero. My favourite example is in *The Return of the Jedi* when Luke has been given a beating by his dad. As Darth is walking about the room saying how Luke should join him in mischief, Luke is hiding in the shadows with half his face in light and the other in darkness. It's a brilliantly simple way in which Luke's good side of the force is set against the dark side – illustrated via a bit of simple side-lighting to show that the two co-exist in him.

- Backlighting comes next. This is when a light, artificial or otherwise, is placed behind an actor and creates a silhouette effect. This is bad if you are filming a news reader, but good if you are introducing some enigmatic baddie into your film.

One important and obvious point to make here as regards the above lighting methods, is the light itself. For example, if you are trying to side-light someone who is standing outside on a very bright sunny day, using a torch isn't going to work. The above lighting effects all rely on some amount of darkness existing to be effective. So, if you are filming in a room that has a lot of natural light coming into it, and you want to place a light under someone's face to make them look nasty, you will have to darken the room in some way – thick black sheets over the window would work.

Don't approach your first day's filming without ever having switched on your lights. Experiment with them, see what effects you can achieve and generally find out the best way to use them.

These effects are all very well for the individuals in your film, but what about the set itself? For the set, a **key light** is placed in a position that will light up as much of the set as possible, and then 'fill lights' are used to fill in the gaps. This method gives a very standard well-lit look, but not everyone will want something like this. A little experimentation is all it takes to make your set more interesting. For example, imagine you are starting with a room that is pitch black. If you were to stick a light behind an open door then, depending on how bright it was, you would get a very dramatic shaft of light striking the room. Alternatively, you could position the lights so that one end of the room was in darkness and the other in light, so when someone walked from the far side of the room, they would emerge from the shadows. Very effective! Just experiment and you will soon find that your lights are an essential component to the film-making montage. They may not be as cool looking as your camera, but if you don't use any, your film will either be in complete darkness or dull. Try to keep the light levels and positions constant during a scene, or when you finish your film the light levels will look haywire as each shot changes in a scene.

Using a monitor

Using a monitor helps you to see whether what you are filming looks the way it should, for example: Is the light OK? Is the guy holding the microphone in shot? Is the colour good? Has the top of the actor's head been cut off?

Although video cameras have small colour or black and white viewfinders, it is recommended that you use a colour monitor. Broadcast cameras use monitors when they can, but you can improvise with a small portable television if you are using a camcorder. All you need to do is obtain a small colour television that plugs into your camera. This way, you will have a full colour view of what your camera is seeing, and you can make lighting adjustments or other changes accordingly. Obviously this isn't always possible outdoors.

In the case of film cameras, however, this is not possible. So what are your options?

a Cross your fingers and hope that everything's OK.
b Have a camcorder in tandem, hooked up to a monitor to give a good idea of the lighting.
c Have someone operating your camera who knows it inside out.

In large scale film productions option (c) is *always* assumed, and option (b) is popular as well. These days the director usually has a broadcast camera filming alongside their 35 mm (or a 35 mm camera that has a video feed) and views the results on a monitor (also some film cameras will have an electronic monitor or attachments for a monitor). Since they are using cassettes, playback is possible. However, this is normally done to see how the action looked, because the lighting and camera people on these big-budget films know *exactly* what they are doing.

Health and safety

Wires, cables and leads are probably the biggest potential source of accidents on your film. If they are not properly attended to people can trip over them and cause the lights they are attached to to fall and break. If you have a lot of cables and leads, try to bunch them all together and have them along the side wall of the room where no one is going to trip over them. However, if they need to go across the floor, bunch them together and then cover them with a piece of heavy material (like an old carpet piece) so it forms a 'bridge' people can walk over.

Bottom-line rules of lights

- Think about your film and assess critically what you are going to need in terms of look, mood and effects. You may discover that you can use one type of light for the whole project and several different effects.

- Like many things when making a film: keep it simple. Lights are one of the 'danger zones' where you could find yourself spending time and energy on getting seriously confused!

- Try to use a monitor where possible. After a while you'll be able to tell how closely the viewfinder matches up with what's on the television screen, as sometimes the edges of the viewfinder's pictures might not appear on the television.

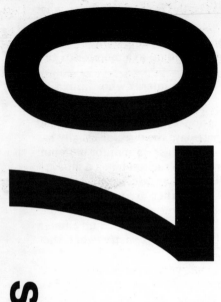

07

sound

In this chapter you will learn:
- how vital sound is to your film and film making
- how to maximize the resources you have
- how sound can be used to enhance and improve your film.

Can you hear what they're saying?

When you are at the cinema, there are two basic things you observe: the images and the sound. Just as the human eye is far superior to a camera at seeing things in different levels of light, the same can be said of the human ear in the context of sound gathering.

Stop for a moment and listen. Chances are that all is silent to your ear or, if there is some sound, your ears are filtering it into something manageable. If you had a camcorder and recorded the same 'silence' using the built-in microphone, then this 'silence' might be a hissing din. Therefore, when you are filming a scene it is important to ensure that you record only the sound you want. So how is this done?

Things to bear in mind

Your chosen camera equipment and where you decide to film will normally dictate what options are open to you. If, for example, you are using a camcorder, or any other video system with a built-in sound recording feature, then the sound from a person speaking in a quiet room will be acceptable. If, however, you are outside on a busy street with strong winds blowing, then that person's voice will be just one feature of the recorded sound and, as such, might seriously compromise things. With built-in microphones it is important to ensure the following:

1 The person/people speaking are relatively close to the microphone.
2 The environment you are in is quiet or sheltered from other 'audio distractions'.
3 The person/people speaking project their voices if necessary.
4 Any wind is blocked from blowing into the microphone (an umbrella, or filming around a corner is good for this).
5 You have some earphones plugged into the camera so you can gauge the quality of the sound – this is a must for *all* sound recordings!

Although many video camera systems have built-in microphones, some have an option that allows you to plug in a lead from an external microphone and point it at whoever is speaking. Therefore, your sound recording needn't be dictated by the distance of the camera from what you are filming. Thus, sound will be very clear and, because the sound is being recorded simultaneously with the images on the video cassette, you won't have to worry about dubbing when editing.

However, if you are using an **external microphone** in a windy environment then you will have to **gag** it. You've all seen gags – they look like furry animals that have been skewered on the end of a microphone. This is a very effective, though not brilliant method of insulating the microphone from the harsh tones of 20 mph winds. A popular term for these in television is a 'Dougal', named after the big hairy dog in *The Magic Roundabout*. External microphones, or **plug-in microphones**, are good for the simple fact that you can manoeuvre them to the best possible position for recording sound in relation to the actors who are speaking, instead of relying on the microphone in the camera.

With film you will always need to record the sound separately, unless the film has magnetic strips on the side, but even then, the sound is going to be a bit ropey. You will therefore need some separate sound recording equipment. How can we improvise in this case?

How to improvise sound recording equipment

You can still find some Walkmans that have a recording capability. If it is possible to plug in a microphone, then this is one way of doing things. If you can't plug it in, then simply put the Walkman near to the actors (in a concealed place where the sound will be picked up). However, Walkmans with this feature may not sound too great when played back, and a serious down side of using them is that very often the playback includes the sound of the Walkman's internal mechanisms.

Some stereo cassette players allow microphones to be plugged in, some don't, so the options, and drawbacks, are as above.

If you have a camcorder, use it to film alongside your film camera. This way you will have the images on the film camera, while your camcorder will have images *and* sound. You can then use the images of the camcorder recording to match up the sound with the film images later on when you dub the dialogue.

If you want to improvise a **boom,** then simply gaffer-tape the microphone to the end of a broom handle or a pole. Make sure that the wire is considerably longer than the boom and that you don't include it when filming. How many times have you seen one hovering above people's heads in a film?

Continuity

As mentioned previously with lighting, you should pay special attention to the continuity of your sound. It is one of the things that can cause unpleasant problems when you are trying to piece your film together.

I think there is always an assumption in today's world, complete with the cameras that boast fully automatic features, that all is taken care of and all you have to do is hold the camera. This, alas, is not the case. I have often observed many first-time film makers just pointing their camera at things, not even considering to listen to the quality of the sound by using headphones. I know of an access documentary that was made for a satellite channel about a police force somewhere in the United States and the majority of the filming was done with mini-DV cams. Although the images were OK, considering they were filming at night, the sound was horrendous. The mini-DV camera teams were more interested in getting the pictures and didn't bother to monitor the sound. The result was that it took some serious high-tech sound engineering to get the recorded sound to understandable levels – and all through want of putting on the headphones!

Wild tracks

A vital way to ensure that your sound continuity is taken care of is to record a **wild track**. Before I explain what a wild track is, I had better tell you why it is needed. As you know, a film is made up of scenes that consist of many different shots which have been filmed at different times instead of in one long run of the camera. This way of working can lead to lapses in continuity, not only with the basic visual elements of the scene, such as people's clothes changing, their positions in a shot or the lighting, but there can also be continuity problems with the soundtrack.

Imagine a scenario where you are filming a basic scene with two people talking. Now there is only one camera, so you will have to film the **mastershot** (the main referencing shot that covers both the actors), followed by the **close-up**, or medium close-up on the individual actors. So you have at least three different runs with which to film your scene and three different chances to obtain three different background sounds that will severely mess up your work.

For example, say you are filming a mastershot in a room and the actors are acting away merrily. Somewhere outside there are some roadworks going on which the microphone is happily picking up (believe me, they can pick up a fly breathing). So, with the first run of the camera you have the mastershot, the corresponding dialogue and the rattling of a pneumatic drill. Now it's time to film the close-up shots on Actor A. This is done and the roadworks have stopped but the microphone picks up a passing jet (this always happens to everyone!). Finally, it is time to film Actor B and the scene is filmed without any distracting noises. Now imagine it is some time later and it is time to put it all together in the edit. This is what would happen:

Shot	Dialogue	Background sound
Mastershot	Thank you for coming Richard.	Pneumatic drill
Actor B	No problem, glad to help.	Silence
Mastershot	OK, let's get to it.	Pneumatic drill
Actor A	Like I said over the phone, this is big.	Passing jet
Actor B	Yeah, a lot of people want this money.	Silence
Actor A	Tell me about it.	Passing jet
Mastershot	So what's the plan?	Pneumatic drill

and so on.

If you were watching a scene like this, it would be dire and there would be nothing you could do about it short of filming the scene again. Now this is quite an extreme and overt example to illustrate a true sound disaster, but the rule here is to make sure that it's quiet when you start filming. 'Silence on set' is not just said to be cool you know!

So what do you do if you are filming outside on a busy street, where there's no escaping the noise? Although you may think that the sound will be fairly constant and uniform, you would be very wrong. If the same three-shot scene was being filmed on a street corner with the corresponding traffic sounds, then another problem would present itself in the edit. Allowing for not recording when a police car with sirens blazing goes past during the mastershot, or the beeping of the pedestrian crossing during the close-up shots on Actor B, you will end up with sound hiccups in the finished scene:

Shot	Dialogue	Sound
Mastershot	So let's go do this.	Background traffic rumble

Jolt!

| Actor B | OK, keep your eyes open. | Background traffic rumble |

Jolt!

| Mastershot | You got the keys to this place? | Background traffic rumble |

Jolt!

| Actor A | Sure. | Background traffic rumble |

Jolt!

and so on.

What has happened here is that at the instant when one shot is linked up with another in the edit, the pitch and tone of the rumbling noises of the traffic jolts slightly, but enough to be noticed. Since the sound of the traffic changes in pitch and tone from second to second, it won't always link up nicely with the shot immediately after it. So what do you do? You record a wild track.

This is essentially a guard against the above problem entering every scene you film. A wild track is a sound-only recording of the **ambient** noise around a scene. In the above example it would be the sounds of a busy street with all the traffic etc. So if you were using your video camera, you would simply hit the record button and point the microphone (built-in or external) in a manner that allows it to best pick up the sounds you are after. This means that in the edit, the jolts and glitches will be masked and smoothed over – the finer technical points of editing such a manoeuvre will be discussed later in the book.

Recording a wild track is a practice you should get into the habit of using. Even if you are in an environment you think is silent –

be it a field on a calm day or the top of a lonely mountain – there will always be some background noise. Hark back to the three-shot example inside the room. Without a wild track, each shot would have a crude 'sound glue-mark' letting everyone know that shots with different sound tones had been stuck together.

You may find yourself filming a scene where your characters are required to watch a television programme. One sound suggestion would be to film the scene without the television switched on, and then record the sound of a television programme. However, due to copyright problems (see page 158) it may be better to record the sound of some people just mumbling to simulate the sound of a television programme playing in the background – although more commonly, in films and television dramas, the sound of gun shots and police sirens are used to serve this function.

There are many fun things to record to add a bit more life and colour to your scenes. You may find yourself in a room with a grandfather clock. This is a lovely warm and atmospheric sound to include. So, as before, film the various shots of the scene without the sound of the thudding pendulum, and then record a wild track afterwards. Actually, a swinging pendulum going unnoticed when filming is very representative of the great 'terrorists' of film making. It is not a sound as noticeable as a pneumatic drill but, if ignored, the edited scene may have turned the gentle thud of the pendulum into something sounding like a disjointed disco beat. Another advantage of recording the sound of something is that you will be able to use it throughout your film, and future productions, as and when you need it.

Sound effects

I hope the above examples have piqued your mind into thinking about recording your own sound effects. Some of them are very easy to improvise. For example, once in an edit suite I suddenly realized that I needed the sound of feet running up stairs as I cut to an exterior of a castle. Since I did not have a sound-effect tape or CD to hand, I simply got a microphone, put it on the ground and did some on-the-spot jogging. The result was brilliant and totally fooled everyone. To improvise a heart beat, simply tap the microphone with your finger in rhythmic, repetitive fashion. It is so easy.

Many professional sound recordists go out into the great outdoors and collect their own real sound effects. For example, they will go into the woods and record the sound of the wind blowing through the leaves on the trees, or the sound of a flowing brook, or maybe a busy street, a train in motion and a dog barking. The advantage of this is that the sounds are their copyright. Sound effects tapes and CDs need special permission and payment before you are allowed to use them in a professional commercial film, as they are owned by someone else. So get out there and record the sounds of the world!

The complexity of the edit method and the technology you use (see page 150) will limit the amount of audio you can have in your edit. For example, the most basic edit method will only allow you to include the dialogue and maybe one sound effect (not at the same time) instead of dialogue and five sound effects (see page 150 for sound in editing).

It is often said by sound recordists that sound is the element of filming that directors pay least attention to. They say that directors can sometimes think that the sound will 'follow on' and be OK in the overall finished product. However, films can be totally ruined by the director not having a basic awareness and consideration of the sound.

Other nightmares that may confront you when filming in certain locations can be the sheer poor overall sound quality. One common problem if you are using a camcorder without a facility for a plug-in microphone, is that if you wish to film two actors speaking and want to arrange the shot so that the actors are far away from the camera, then you are not going to hear a thing anyone is saying. A cheat device commonly used in these situations is simply to record the actors' dialogue separately and then put it in when you get to the edit. You will then have your lovely shot, say, of two people walking across the brow of a hill as the sun goes down, and still be able to clearly hear everything they say. Also, that they will be too far away for anyone to notice their lips aren't in sync!

Although this chapter deals with sound, I realize that I'm starting to introduce techniques from the editing process as it helps a great deal when filming if you have an appreciation of the post-production process.

Overcoming problems

Get into the habit of filming and recording with half a mind on what 'problems' a particular scene may present in the edit. For everyday examples of how the above problems have been remedied, take a look at news reports. Although you may feel that these are an unlikely source of film-making knowledge, you would be very wrong.

Every day news teams have to get stories out within a deadline and they are not usually in an environment where they can arrange re-shoots. There is a general 'formula' that news crews use when interviewing people, and it is the relation of techniques used in any film you see in the cinema. It generally goes like this:

person – cutaway – person – cutaway – person

Whenever you watch someone being interviewed in a news report, what you are generally seeing is maybe a 45-second edited version of something that may have taken several minutes to film. This is because if the interviewee says something that is not required, this has to be left out of the report. So how is this done without causing a jolt in the sound and picture?

Cutaways

Have a look at this imagined news feature:

> Shot 1 – Person is answering third question.
> Shot 2 – Cutaway of sheep in a field.
> Shot 3 – Person is answering fifth question.

So what the **cutaway** has done is to *mask* two different discontinuous shots that would otherwise cause a jump cut (see page 110) *and* it has taken your attention away from any jolt in the sound. Very simple and very effective.

This is a variation of the mastershot example earlier, but instead of filming and recording the sound from more than one set-up, it is only the *shot* that varies. Next time you watch a feature film or television film drama, look out for a scene where two people are having a conversation. There will usually be a cutaway taken from a distance – it's the more eloquent relation of the news rush-job.

Once again I refer to Robert Rodriguez and his ten-minute film school. He constantly talks about making editing decisions in the middle of the actual process of filming. This not only saves time in the edit process (as there is less to sift through), but it also means that things are filmed more quickly as you know how you want it stuck together later and need only film what you have to.

I'm straying into the world of camera work and techniques here, but it illustrates how intricately connected the basic filming processes are – they are all part of the same whole. What happens with one process has repercussions for the rest, so get it right!

Microphone settings

Some of the digital video cameras that are available these days not only have a plug-in microphone socket fitted as standard, but will have a facility that enables you to manipulate your recording levels. The two basic settings for recording levels are: **automatic** and **manual**. No surprise there. But how does this translate into uses in your film?

Automatic setting

A camera that has its sound recording function switched over to automatic constantly monitors all the sounds it registers and finds a mid-level. This is a good system to have when you are in an environment with constant predictable sounds, for example, two people having a conversation (again!) in a room where there is a steady rumble of traffic outside. This is an ideal set up, and the recorded sound will also be at a constant level with a good overall quality. Even if you were filming the crowd at a football match, a mid-point would be found and you'd have a decent sound level.

The only time when automatic recording levels are a drawback is when there is a sudden change in the sound level. So, imagine that the same two actors are having a dialogue while standing by

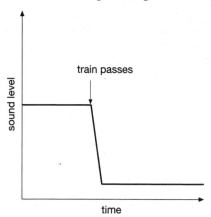

figure 6

a level-crossing and a train rushes by. What will happen here is that the sound record facility will think, 'Oh my Lord, that's loud! Let's turn things down.' So when played back your shot will have the words from the dialogue, and then when the train rushes past the overall recorded sound level will steeply drop to a significantly lower level. Professional sound recordists call this phenomenom 'falling off the cliff' and it may help to imagine the sound level as a line (see Figure 6).

The most common situation where automatic sound levels cause problems is in scenes where there are gun shots. I've known a few occasions when people have filmed a great-looking gun fight scene, only to play it back on a monitor or in an edit suite and find that the sound of the first gun shot suddenly drops to almost nothing half way through, and the rest of the shots sound about as loud as someone punching a pillow.

Again, these are extreme examples to illustrate a point. However, I hope it has highlighted a downside of the automatic function. By being aware of what your recording environment will be like, you can easily avoid this problem. Actually, automatic is the preferred way of doing things. When taking a camera out filming, I've often been told: 'Just leave it on automatic mate.'

Manual setting

Having the option of a manual setting does have its own uses. Using the passing train example, Figure 7 shows what would happen if the camera was set to manual.

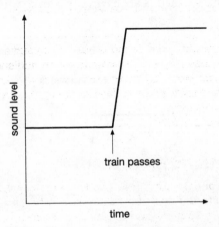

figure 7

Since the camera's sound facility has been adjusted only for the relatively low-volume experience of two people's voices, the passing train will sound much louder and therefore it will turn the recorded sound into something that sounds like an atomic bomb blast. Manual sound is set at a certain level to record only sound from *that* level, for example, something softer will be hard to hear and something much louder will end up being a distorted din.

The gun shot example given earlier is a very good example of when to use manual sound. Using this, you could keep the levels high so that the bangs would sound like bangs. It can also be a good way of distorting things so that you can achieve the sort of effect you may want to go with your scene and film. For example, you may need to simulate a distorted radio message from a spaceship in distress.

Manual sound is a rather tricky thing to master overnight. It needs constant tweaking and monitoring to get it right, as the volume of someone's voice will be changing constantly depending on the emotional content of the scene, and also the ambient sound of certain locations will present their own problems. Trying to adjust things manually throughout a camera run could end up with your soundtrack being alternately inaudible or too loud and distorted. Also, many DV cams will require that you stop recording to access the manual sound level control. So this would be impractical.

However, the advantage comes from the fact that in excessively loud or soft audio situations you can adjust the levels better than you could ever achieve on automatic. Think of the manual level as a guard for the more extreme sound situations.

A bad picture with good sound is easy on an audience. A good picture with bad sound is frustrating for an audience. Case in point: Michael Moore's *Bowling for Columbine* has some unlit footage filmed at dusk; the images are barely visible, but perfect sound saves the day.

Radio microphones

Radio microphones are rather handy things to get hold of. Just like other external microphones they can be connected, via a receiver, to a camera and allow you a certain amount of flexibility regarding your filming options. You can, for example, move your camera around without having to worry about getting tangled up in the sound recordist's leads. You can also film a bit further away without having to think where to hide the external microphone and so on. You can hire these microphones relatively cheaply from a community camera hire outlet. They are best used in long shots, as they can eradicate the need for making a separate sound recording of the dialouge. Basically they allow you to record sound from people who are a considerable distance from the camera.

However, a few words of warning: they eat up batteries like there's no tomorrow, so when not in use, switch them off and make sure they are disconnected.

When I worked for a shopping channel it wasn't unknown for an off-air presenter to be heard over the air going to the toilet as their colleagues were talking about Teflon cooking utensils. Radio mics have also been known to pick up the odd tummy rumble and stifled belch. When the microphones rub against clothes, they can create a very awkward and noticeable sound. Make sure they are concealed, otherwise they will ruin your scene.

Sound recording tip

If filming next to a busy road you can reduce, but not eradicate, the sound of the traffic by using the bodies of the actors as 'sound blocks' by appropriate framing and positioning of the micro- phone. For example, if the microphone is close enough to the body, and away from the traffic, the body will shield the microphone from the sound of all the cars (see Figure 8). This technique is used by news reporters the world over.

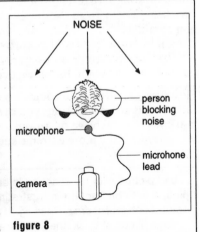

figure 8

Professional sound recording equipment is available from the same outlets as the cameras. The staff should be very willing to answer any questions you may have about the equipment. A popular lightweight system you might want to ask about is DAT (Digital Audio Tape). However, from my experience the best, easiest and most effective way of recording sound is via an external microphone. This is because:

1 The microphone can be manoeuvred to a good recording position (providing it's out of shot!).

2 Since the sound is being recorded on the tape in synchronization with the images, there are no dubbing nightmares when editing. This is why films use a clapper board which acts as a reference point in the edit, so that the sound can be synchronized with the images – when the clapper board goes 'snap', the dubber can link up the 'snap!' on the screen with the 'snap!' on the sound recording.

Bottom-line rules of sound

- Always use earphones or headphones, otherwise you won't have a clue how good or bad the sound is.

- Think about the sort of filming situations you are going to be in and assess what kind of microphone you will need. (Just because there are several different kinds of microphones available does not mean that you will need to use each one.)

- If you are only able to use a system that has an on-board microphone then don't worry, just pay very close attention to how you can maximize the sound it records.

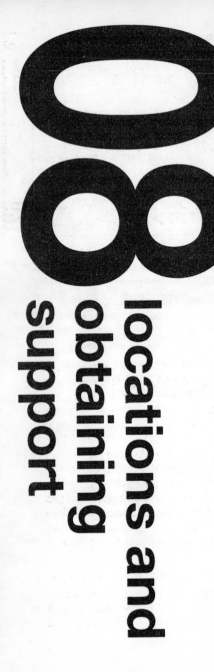

08
locations and obtaining support

In this chapter you will learn:
- how to find or 'make' locations that will fit your film
- the importance of viewing locations prior to filming at them
- how locations can help get your film some official sponsorship.

Your equipment is all ready, but there's just one problem – you've got nowhere to film. Location is just one of the many things that you will have to sort out before those cameras start rollin'. So how do you decide in what kind of places you would like to film? The answer lies in the script.

There are probably a few broad bandings when it comes to the kind of locations your script will be calling for. Genre is the key element of your script and story and will influence the sort of places you look out for. For example, a crime thriller would be well suited to city environments – secret meetings taking place under bridges, in downtown pubs and bars, streets and so forth. A sci-fi storyline would need industrial complexes (such as the quiet corners of oil refineries – *Red Dwarf* always used this); wide-open and desolate places such as a beach far from built-up areas, and an old open-cast mine is always a good substitute for an alien planet, especially when used in conjunction with a filter over the camera lens. An historic script would of course need period buildings – both exteriors and interiors.

Be realistic

When writing the script it is always wise to be mindful of the limitations that may be presented by an ambitious story. There is little point in writing numerous and marvellous scenes set in fantastic places if obtaining such locations proves impossible due to the factors of expense, distance and the realization that such places do not exist (unless purpose-built). Try to think of locations as limiters to your story and script. Being aware of what is available and tenable to your production will allow you to set scenes and action in places that you know you will be able to get hold of. I know of individuals who have composed scripts without taking the above considerations on board and then moaned when they discovered they were not allowed to run riot through the local five-star hotel or some other important building.

That said, as with many things in the film-making process, there is usually some way of improvising what you are trying to get hold of. Your ability to think laterally and be resourceful may save the day with regard to getting hold of your otherwise impossible and fantastic location.

Improvise your setting

So consider a script that opens up like this:

> **EXT: Aircraft Carrier. Landing deck – Day**
>
> The sea is extremely rough and the aircraft are preparing for take-off.

This might be a tricky one to arrange. You will therefore have to think of a substitute that conveys the same feeling. You could rig up a glass window and the area immediately behind it to look the part, with charts, aircraft diagrams, someone suitably attired looking out with a pair of binoculars, etc. You could also move the camera back and forth rhythmically and occasionally spray water at the window. In the edit you could put in the appropriate sounds. Think laterally and approach a complicated location from another route. Now think about some more complicated locations mentioned in a script and see what you can come up with. For example:

> **EXT: Battle field – Day**
>
> Explosions detonate and shots whistle near to a group of huddled troops.

Here you could have a trench in a field somewhere. The shot would help if it was quite close in. Shaking the camera once in a while would simulate a bomb exploding nearby and a bit of loose dirt chucked in time with the camera shake could represent debris which has been thrown up. The more ambitious of you might devise some way of creating smoke. You could also zoom into the distance and go in and out of focus to simulate the soldiers desperately and frantically looking through their rifle sights at the unseen enemy. You could also do a few blurred **whip pans** (see page 170) to simulate bullets flying through the air.

> **EXT: Desert planet – Day**
>
> A lone figure walks across the expanse of the sand sea.

This is one of my favourites as it's so simple to achieve, but it does help to have a beach nearby – and preferably one where the tide goes out so far that it does actually resemble a desert. To trick the audience, use a red or orange filter which will instantly give your shots that 'off-world' look. Filming from a low angle towards the sun will further accentuate the heat of the place. Although having a beach where the tide goes out for a very long way is a luxurious way of filming such a trick, any rocky and sandy area will suffice – even a quarry, just so long as the picture is framed in a manner that excludes anything that will ruin the shot, such as a wall or a truck.

The smaller the location, the tighter the shot will have to be, but this will lend a strange sense of claustrophobia to the situation (more about framing later). Also, you will have to film things from as many different angles as possible due to the small size of the area. One trick of the trade is to light some fire lighters (the sort used for barbeques) and place them in front of the camera. Now zoom through the 'invisible' flame and you've got instant heat shimmer – even if it is a mid-winter's day. However, know where this 'invisible' flame is so that you don't burn your camera. The best example of using this heat effect is in the film *Dune* by David Lynch. There is a scene where the Royal Family arrives on Dune and the entire clip is given an almost unbearable 'shot' of heat using this method – so effective you can almost feel it.

These examples are probably not what everyone will want to film, but they do reveal how settings can be effectively improvised by using different resources.

Inexpensive/free locations

So your script includes many things: story, characters and settings. The settings are the places you will need to find or recreate. For many reasons a lot of people choose to film low-budget films in their own or their friends' houses. The reason for this 'cottage industry' is that you have unlimited permission and access; you can do what you want (within reason); everyone you work with will probably know how to get there (ease of access) and it is free (biggest advantage). People's bedrooms, or rooms of a house in general, are great starting points for a low- or no-budget film.

By looking at a script you will see that there are probably a few scenes that take place in rooms. If it were the room of our private detective friend, Richard Vincent, then you could start off with just a desk, chair and window – maybe even just a desk and chair. The window could be blacked out and the room lit in a suitably 'crime-like' manner to emphasize the nether world that this fellow inhabits. Simple, sparse props can give a room great 'direction' and be very effective in illustrating a point in the film. For example, a room decked out to be somewhere in an embassy might need only a flag and a framed picture of a President or Prime Minister to tell the audience 'what's going on'. Start with the basics and then, if necessary, work your way up. Remember: *keep it simple*. This goes for all aspects of the film-making process.

You could even use the same room for a multitude of scenes simply by filming from another angle and altering the furniture and props. With such a set-up, many of the cutaways and single shot scenes can be put out of the way in relatively little time. Rooms are an amazing little-known-about resource, so make sure you can get hold of a few. Who knows, maybe your entire film could be shot in a series of rooms.

While on the subject of cheap/free resources, have a think of others that may be available to you. Public places such as parks, the countryside, the beach, a forest etc. are all calling out for you to use them. They are all free, so see if you can fit them in somewhere. One point to bear in mind, though, is that although free, you may need to obtain permission to film there depending on what you are going to get up to exactly. So when musing over how nice the local park is, or how suitable the grounds of the local museum would be for the final scene of your film, be very aware that such a place is owned and there will be a specific department of local council or wherever that you need to approach before you proceed further. *Never* assume that it will be OK to turn up somewhere and start filming a few scenes. Plan for everything and look into everything – don't leave anything to chance. Your local *Yellow Pages* will list the department of parks and leisure (in the instance of a park scenario), so phone them in advance and explain what it is you want to do.

Use friends and their contacts to find some great locations. I once discovered, through the course of a conversation about locations, that the person I was speaking to had a brother who managed the bridges of Prague. I was told that, if I wanted,

I could get the famous Charles Bridge cordoned off for free! It just goes to show that a lot comes down to, 'peripheral and lateral resources and opportunities'.

Once again, it is very important to know what category your intended production is going to fall into when trying to arrange permission to film in public places, as well as with many other aspects of making a film. This is because you will be asked if you are a professional/commercial company or an educational/community project. If you are a professional/commercial company then you are more likely to be charged a fee for using the park (or wherever) than if you state that you are an educational/community-level organization. The best/worst example I know of was when I was doing some pre-production work on an experimental Gothic-type film based in London. I stumbled across a magnificent location which used to be a cathedral and was now used as a public forum for community arts 'happenings'. It was huge, cavernous and Gothic and looked perfect for the throne room for one of the characters in the script. Sadly I approached the situation all wrong. When I met up with the man who managed the site I introduced myself as being from a film company (I was just a private citizen), which made him think, 'Great – money!' When we got around to arranging filming, I thought it would just be a case of saying 'when' and then turning up since it was a free community resource. This was not the case. Since I said I was from a film company (just to sound credible) he quoted me a huge figure. It was an impossible figure to work with and, by the time I explained it was really just a small-scale community production, it was too late and he wouldn't budge on the price. So for the sake of wanting to sound 'Mr Hollywood', I blew a unique location. I was never to make that mistake again! Remember: be realistic and be honest.

The size of your film is something to which you should always give serious thought. It may be hard, at first, to determine where things are going, but after finalizing the script, you may have a rough idea of what resources you intend to use. This consideration ties in very closely with the funding side of things (see page 97), but don't go making your location arrangements on the proviso that there will be a big stash of money at your disposal somewhere down the line.

Film makers and those involved with television dramas and other programmes don't just flatly accept a fee for filming somewhere. It seems that owners of stately homes and country parks think these 'glamorous' people have bags of money ready to throw at anyone who quotes them a high price. They often find out it's the other way around. If a price for a location is too high the film/programme makers will either go elsewhere or try to negotiate a lower fee. It's a practice you should employ. Look for what's free, and if it's not free see if you can get some kind of deal. If you still can't reach an agreement, look elsewhere.

Visit your location

Once you have nailed down your location it is very important to take a 'recce'. A recce is a look around the location to establish a few basic facts about it:

- How easy is it to get there (public transport or camel train)?
- How large is it (will it accommodate everyone with the equipment)?
- Is it safe (floors, walls, electrics...)?
- What facilities does it have (several plug sockets, toilets)?
- What permission is required?
- What is the layout like (so you can start thinking about your shots)?
- What are its opening times (if applicable)?

And so on and so forth.

This is just another example of the preparation you should be aware of when making a film. There is nothing worse than turning up to film somewhere only to discover that there is nowhere to plug the lights in, or that it is closed on that particular day. All these things do happen! The most common and horrendous oversights usually occur with foreign locations. Stories abound of film crews being booked into hotels, flights arranged, cameras hired, film stock bought in, permissions granted etc., only to discover on arrival that the country is having a major religious holiday and all the places that are required to be filmed are totally shut down. *The biggest disasters are caused by the smallest oversights.* Get to know your locations well – they are, after all, the silent actors in your film.

Consideration for others

Another consideration to bear in mind is any 'disturbances' you may cause. Some may be irresponsible on many levels. For starters, having the public walk by seeing people pointing guns at each other is not very smart. It may cause distress to some people, some may be seriously spooked and others driving past in cars may be distracted to the point where a crash may occur. Added to this, the police may not look too kindly on such things. Having your lead arrested due to a lack of planning and downright irresponsibility is not a great way to make films.

Always make sure that your actions do not inconvenience others. Depending on how large your film crew will be, you should plan accordingly. Just you with a camcorder filming someone walking on the other side of the street will probably go unnoticed. However, something involving lights, a larger camera and actors saying their lines will be very noticeable. Tell shop owners politely that you may be filming outside their shop next week or whenever, and try not to get in people's way too much. It's just a case of simple planning and awareness on your part. If your script has a shoot-out scene in it, not only will you have to tell the local shop owners, residents and so forth, but you will have to notify the local police station well in advance. I don't have to explain what would happen if your actors went go around with noisy blank-firing guns. Just have some courtesy and common sense!

Location tip

If suited to your script, think about filming on public transport. Although these locations may seem rather inconspicuous and dull, they are great as you can have a couple of people acting while out of the window things are going by which will give the scene a great deal of energy for a minimum amount of effort on your part.

From reading through the script it will be obvious what scenes require what type of location. However, you might not always be allowed to film somewhere you have your heart set on. The script excerpt given on page 12 was set first in a street and then in a bank. With that example in mind, you will realize that it isn't as problematic to film something on a street – so long it's not too busy – as it is to film in a bank. Turning up unannounced with your cameras and thespians in tow is a big no-no. The answer to the above locational problem would be to:

a ask permission from the bank
b improvise elsewhere.

Usually the solution will be 'b' (unless, of course, the bank manager is a frustrated actor and hopes for a part – happens quite a bit, you know). Here are a few alternatives:

• a library
• a room with a table and 'Bank' written on the wall
• an area of a school
• a university information area
• a university reception area
• most business reception areas
• an area educational office
• somewhere in a council building.

A bit of brain storming, lateral thinking and imagination is all that is needed to come up with alternative venues.

I once made a film where several scenes were set in the fictitious MI6 offices of the British Embassy in Prague. Since my fledgling film empire was based in a living room and I had intended originally to film everything in the local area, it would have been pointless to try to attempt to gain permission to film in the actual place as stipulated in the script. I put my thinking cap on and thought of the largest property owner in the area – the local council. They own lots of lovely buildings from Victorian town halls to burnt-out houses. Quite a varied choice. (Some local councils and offices even have their own public relations departments or actual film departments to help films get made in the area; although you may find that film offices only like to get involved with 'big and prestigious' projects.)

I rang the council's head office and arranged a meeting with one of the councillors. At the meeting I basically repeated what I had said to him on the phone, only in much more detail, and listened to his ideas. He recommended that I contact the manager of the local town hall. This I did and, after making an appointment, was led into a place called the Mayor's Parlour Room – a huge, exquisite room full of grandiose furnishings, pictures of the Queen and Prince Philip, William Morris wallpaper etc. I was immediately hooked on the idea of using it for the MI6 offices in the British Embassy in Prague. The manager then informed me that it would cost a certain amount a day to hire. I explained that the project was a non-profit community film involving students and young people in general. After hearing this he said, 'OK, it's yours to use for a maximum of seven days, not including weekends.'

I requested a letter from him laying out what we had just agreed, so that:

a I had official proof of his offer, and
b other organizations, be they arts funding bodies or whoever, would see that I was genuinely making a film.

I now had sponsorship *in kind*, i.e. sponsorship that does not relate to money, but assistance and help in general. Having such a letter is essential if you wish to go to arts funding bodies for finance. The reason for this is that organizations who hand out money insist that the arts practitioner (you) is making an effort to get support for the film underway, rather than just approaching them and asking for some cash! I cannot stress how important such letters and supporting documentation are in the process of getting thos *readies* ready.

The official budget for this film was tens of thousands. About three quarters of that was sponsorship in kind – it only existed on paper.

Here are a few other suggestions of places you could contact for possible locations:

• the local health authority
• the local educational authority (including schools and colleges)
• community centres
• local estate agents
• local parks and nature reserves.

The potential list is very, very long. They don't always have to be official buildings; you could ask the local restaurant, a farm and so on. Don't forget that letter stating that they are prepared to let you film there for free, whereas the normal cost of hiring out the place for the time you want it would be a certain price, cost or rate.

Useful tip

Try to ensure that your letters of support are typed on headed paper from the organization or business you've approached, otherwise anyone could have written them.

The more places you can think of, the greater the potential for getting those lovely letters of support. It doesn't only have to relate to locations; you may get some free assistance from a lighting rental company, a caterer, a camera hire outlet and so on. Try to get as many goods and services for free as possible, but always get a letter stating how much this service would normally be valued at.

Bottom-line rules of locations and support

- Be very realistic when thinking of locations.
- Be aware that not everyone will step aside with awe when you tell them you want to film at a certain place. You may need to be convincing in order to change things around.
- Have a look at your chosen place beforehand, don't just assume it will be a good place to film.
- When you have managed to get permission to use a location, get it in writing.

09

financing your film

In this chapter you will learn:
- how to budget accurately for your film
- some potential sources of funding for your film
- what to do if it doesn't go to plan.

Quick recap

Right, before we discuss finance, a short recap on what we have covered so far.

1 Write the script or, at the very least, know what the film is to be about.
2 Sort out your actors and make sure they are reliable and right for the part.
3 Decide what camera system you want to use.
4 Know how to use your chosen camera, or find someone who does.
5 Have an idea of what lights and lighting effects, if any, you want in the film.
6 Figure out how you're going to record your sound, particularly if there are any special considerations to be taken into account.
7 Decide where you are going to film.
8 Obtain permission to film in the places you want.
9 Make some kind of preliminary efforts to get official support for your film.

If you feel confident about the above, it's time to crank up another gear and think about how you are going to finance your film.

How much will all this cost?

Before you start thinking of the many ways you can get money to pay for aspects of your film (that's presuming you need any), you should first think about how much it is going to cost. It is very important to work out some kind of budget for your film, and your finance philosophy should always be, 'Don't pay for something unless there is no other option.'

As highlighted in the previous chapter, if I hadn't been careful I could have ended up paying for the hire of the lovely room in my local town hall at an expensive rate. As it was, I negotiated something. You, too, should try and see what's possible. Then, and *only* then should you consider paying for things – but always try to wangle some kind of discount. You'll be surprised how prices come down when you say you're making a film. When you come into contact with groups and organizations that help out film makers, they will be very aware of the problems you are experiencing, and you won't be the first person who has turned up with cap in hand asking for something for free.

Stop for a moment and consider this logic: to buy and rent things that you need to make your film (depending on its size, of course) calls for money. Obtaining money can be a stressful and tiresome exercise, as this chapter will highlight, so what many first-time and low-budget film makers do is to ignore this problematic issue in the first place.

I'll explain. When you are successful at getting money, you then spend it on renting a camera and kit, for example. Why not consider trying to get hold of the camera and kit for free? Directly target the resource you are after in the first place. As the first chapter states, if you don't ask for something you don't get it. There is a whole world of potentially free and heavily discounted items out there just waiting for you to come along.

For some reason there seems to be a consensus that in order for any kind of film to be made, vast quantities of money must be thrown at it. Remember, making films is often about the art of improvising and making do with whatever resources are immediately available to you. Don't get hung up trying to get that 'magic cheque' that will suddenly green-light your film and allow things to start in the morning. The reality of having the means to go ahead with making your project is rarely a glamorous thing – constantly assess what you have, what you need, and try to find out what the trade-off between the two is. All too often, people feel that they have to reach a certain equipment or finance threshold before they can go ahead with making their film. Remember, film making can be a 'cottage industry'.

Expenses

Let's now discuss the kinds of things you will have to pay for.

Administration

Arranging all of the above, and everything else in this book, does cost money. Not great amounts, but buying printer paper, paying for photocopies, travelling to meetings, paying phone bills, faxes and general office type things do add up. One thing likely to cause a 'cost spike' are phone calls. It takes a lot of phone calls to arrange, research and generally make a film, so beware and be prepared to expect a higher phone bill than normal. After camera hire, phone calls was the second highest cost when I made my first film.

Obviously costs can vary dramatically depending on how 'big' you see your film being.

Camera hire

This will depend on the system you have chosen to work with. You may be able to be borrow camcorders and some other systems from relatives and friends; other formats might not be quite so cheap.

Cassettes or film stock for your camera

It's rather embarrassing turning up on set and realizing that you don't have any film, although I've been on shoots where this has happened! Borrowing or being given second-hand tapes may seem like a good financial move, but this is not the greatest way to achieve high-quality images or sound. However, one popular way of getting reduced-price, or sometimes free, film is to obtain surplus unused film from another production (although trying to find these productions and consequent surplus film is another matter).

Lights

You will need to add these to your budget, but only if you have decided on the more powerful and/or professional lighting systems that are usually hired out by certain companies.

Rental of locations

In the event of a place not giving you permission to film somewhere for free (and no nice letter of support), and if its *absolutely* vital for a particular scene, then you'll have to hire it.

Food and drink

If you don't plan on paying your actors and crew, for the simple reason that you don't think you'll be able to, then you should at least do them the courtesy of feeding them. Having people stand around all day between takes isn't fun at the best of times; having them stand around all day with rumbling stomachs is worse. Don't forget that people can often feel faint under the hot lights, and this, together with an empty stomach, can spell disaster. No one is forcing them to attend, so keep them happy (cheap cafés and sandwich shops will do fine) and make an effort to get on with them – otherwise they may walk out on you.

Travel expenses

As with the above, it's a courtesy that will go a long way to showing the cast and crew that you care. However, make sure you stipulate public transport only, or some smart Alec will turn up in a taxi and hand you the bill.

Additional costs

Depending on what your film is about, how ambitious it is and so on, here are a few things you might want to consider when costing your film:

- make-up
- hairdressing
- special effects
- costumes
- props.

As with previous lists, this is not an exhaustive one and you will no doubt think up some of your own. For example, a period Hammer Horror-type film will involve all of the above, whereas a documentary about a day in an office probably won't. **Important note:** Just because I have listed these things does not necessarily mean that you will have to pay for them. Your powers of negotiation will decide the day! But don't forget those letters of support.

Obtaining funding

Methods for obtaining money range from the simple to the sublime. I only received a few thousand pounds for my first film. You may think that this is peanuts, but what stranger is going to give you that amount of money? So, how and where can you obtain it? Let's take a look at some tried and tested methods.

1 Paying for it yourself

> **Film fact**
> Did you know that George Lucas paid for *The Empire Strikes Back* himself?

Obviously not many people will be capable of such expenditure, but if you have enough savings, and are prepared to spend them on a film, then that's great. If not, then you'll have to try...

2 Asking friends and relatives

A straightforward and simple method. You simply approach them and ask. No doubt some of them, depending on how big your film project is, won't be able to afford to help. Some kindly uncle or aunt may hand out the occasional sum here and there but, on the whole, friends and relatives may, quite rightly, be extremely dubious about handing over their hard-earned money. If this method draws a blank, how about...

3 Approaching local businesses

This is another popular method of financing a film (and lots of other things). This avenue of funding is a form of sponsorship (see point 6) but on a much smaller scale. As such, it may take several 'bites' before you have enough interest and money to start things moving. I know a film that was part sponsored by the local pie shop, and an early Ed Wood film was financed in its entirety by a meat wholesaler. Although perhaps not an obvious choice, the shops and businesses on your high street, or wherever, may be receptive to helping you out. It doesn't hurt to ask!

4 Selling shares in your film

Unlike the above three examples, this has to be a very well planned, well thought out and professionally tailored mode of getting money. Basically what you are doing is selling interest in a business, i.e. your film. The sale of the shares pays for the film, and when the film makes money you pay back the shareholders at a previously agreed percentage. Like all business ventures there is a certain degree of risk involved – the shareholders are not guaranteed any returns. Also, some of them may get cold feet and suddenly decide that they want the value of their shares back. If the film isn't a money spinner, the shareholders may get a tad irate with you.

If you want to pursue this line of fund raising then it would be a good idea to consult a professional (bits of paper with 'Film Share' written on them and sold at street corners will not do). Go to the local business centre, your bank manager, the local film office, etc. and get some sound advice before you even think of getting things under way. Want something riskier? Then try...

5 Paying for it on credit card

Those little oblong pieces of bright plastic have paid for more films than you might think. I've been at film-maker's meetings and heard people talk about their experiences of this type of film financing. A member of a Liverpool film agency suggested that I make my film like this, even though I was unemployed at the time. Obviously it's very risky, but if a credit card is at hand then you can start paying for things right away, such as camera hire, transport or whatever. Now if anyone reading this has a credit card, then you will know how easy it is to spend money without realizing it. 'It's only plastic, there's no cash involved.' Such was the saying of many of my student chums while at university – before a huge credit card bill fell through the letter box with a resounding thud. It's easy to pay for things with a credit card when making a film, but getting that money back to pay the eventual bill is another matter. The best example I can think of where a film was financed by credit card was the low-budget satire *Hollywood Shuffle*, by director Robert Townsend. Luckily for Mr Townsend the film was a big success and started his career.

6 Private sponsorship

Many large businesses and corporations are used to having complete strangers ring them up and ask them for money. In fact, they usually have their own private sponsorship departments.

While making one film I received private sponsorship from two completely unrelated (and possibly unlikely) sources: Bass Beers International and Czech Airlines. Although they didn't actually give me any money, they did save me huge amounts by giving me things for free – thousands of pounds/dollars worth of beer, props and technical assistance, as mentioned before – while Czech Airlines gave me a 70 per cent discount on flights from Manchester to Prague. The latter saved me a few thousand when I eventually took the cast and crew to the Czech Republic. Just because an organizsation won't give you money need not mean that all is lost – remember the logic about avoiding money and going directly for the resource.

Try to be strategic when you are contacting potential sponsors. Think of reasons why they should help you out. Is there any relation between your film and the nature of their business, for example? If your film is about a religious sect who shun alcohol, then it probably isn't a good idea to contact breweries for sponsorship.

7 Arts organizations

A great deal of focus is currently on arts organizations as potential sources of funding for low-budget films – and even some larger ones as well. There are numerous grants, loans and other financial packages operated by these organizations and they are usually very eager to help with advice and assistance in finding information about funding processes and so on. They are often the first port of call for people who have never done a creative project before.

One important thing they will tell you, and something you will see on application forms for money, is the importance of having other sponsors, or **partners**, that are interested in your film. This brings us back to those letters of support. These letters are the building blocks when it comes to obtaining money from national or regional arts organizations. Some grants state that you will need to have some money available, in addition to other support, before you can be considered for a grant payment.

They also won't always pay grants to individuals, which means you will need to call yourself something. This is to make sure that people don't get paid grants and then fly off to Phuket, or wherever, for a year. Most banks and building societies will have club or business accounts that you can set up in the name of your 'company' or film organization so that if you do manage to get a grant, or any other money, you can ask them to pay it to 'Ace Films', instead of Gary Smith, for example. You may be required to open an account with at least two signatories.

Useful tip

Having a company or organization name is a very good way of giving you and your film some credibility, especially when it comes to fund raising. Try to think of a relatively sensible name, as a silly arty name may not be an impressive 'calling card'.

---

8 Charitable trusts

These places exist solely to fund a variety of projects and proposals, from people who want to climb Everest (the hard way) to buying chairs for hospital waiting rooms. To contact them, look up 'The Directory of Grant Making Trusts and Charitable Organizations – 2006' (or whenever) available in most reference libraries. You can also find them in Arts Board offices. These directories list every organization and charity that falls under the criteria for the book, that is, places that give money out and don't ask for it back. There will, quite possibly, be a few thousand listings in the book, but many of them won't be applicable to financing a film. The individual organizations have quite strict guidelines when it comes to receiving and deciding on proposals – and they won't deviate from these rules for anyone. For example, an organization that specializes in giving money to African women so they can study medicine in Europe will not be your best bet. This serves to show just how specific their guidelines can be.

But fear not. There are organizations that give money to the arts, film, video, acting community, drama projects and so forth. It is essential that you consult the subject index in these directories to see whom you should be contacting. Some of these organisations may only have a small annual budget to give away to the arts, while others may have millions. Pay attention to the deadlines for proposal submissions (if any exist), and watch out for those mysterious places that state that they *don't* like to be contacted by telephone, otherwise you could upset a potential sponsor.

Since these organizations, and others mentioned in this section, are often very big bureaucratic labyrinths, it is very important to get a contact name when you first approach them. Without getting the name of someone, it could take a very long time before your enquiry letter, email or voicemail message is registered as lost.

9 Community film and video companies

Once in a while a community organization dealing with the hiring of professional film-making equipment and services will run a bursary. This will be a relatively small amount of money that is occasionally given out to a local film maker whom they class as being a 'non-professional'. A drawback with these is that the subject matter and duration for the bursaries is often quite specific and it isn't a case of being handed some money and then filming what you want with it.

10 Local film agencies

As with point 9, these are grants and schemes aimed at encouraging local talent in film production. They can sometimes be quite non-specific with regard to duration and subject matter and thus tend to be very popular with local low-budget film makers.

11 National Funding

This method of funding has overlaps with the Arts Organizations as well as the Grant Making and Charitable Trust directories, as details and information of their grants will be available from both. Although National Funding has grants comparable to the Arts Boards, they are not targeted at regions. Instead they are, as the name suggests, *national*.

National Funding gives money to lots of different causes but for arts practitioners, including budding film makers, there will be a fair number of grants that apply. The monetary value varies from hundreds to millions and, needless to say, the grant forms that deal with the larger figures are very detailed and complex – they require that you have money-giving partners and the form is a very official-looking document. The grants for smaller amounts are wonderfully simple. However, please realize that with all grant forms you will have to state exactly how much money you want, and *why* you need this much money – refer to the section on costing your film.

A long haul

There are many other sources of funding, from fiddly and complex multi-national funding bodies to a simple small business grant or a local authority scheme. It's worth bearing in mind that a large organization may take a very long time to reach a decision. Don't expect a reply over the phone or within a week of making an application. These things are all reviewed, referred and considered for what seems like an eternity to an impatient film maker. Take this into account when planning things.

As I have highlighted a few times already, it is very important to know how big your production will eventually be. The reason why this has been drummed into you is so that it will not only influence your choice of equipment and so on, but also how much money you may need. If, from having looked over your script and gauging your ambition, you feel that your film is a big production that can only be made successfully with the injection of serious amounts of cash then fine. But...

Trying to obtain large amounts of money to start making your film is a thing that can turn your hair grey and ruin your life – I kid you not. This is why I have droned on about seriously thinking about what *level* your film will be at while trying to instil the importance of being a negotiator. If you realize that you are able to tell your tale effectively with the use of a camcorder, some friends and a small amount of cash, then that's great. A script will 'communicate' to you what level it wants to be filmed at, and you may be mindful of this when you are sitting down writing it. Some of you may think your script will be best served by a bit of casting at the local drama society and by using some professional-grade cameras and equipment. Others will write the script with the solid intention of going the distance with 35 mm film and the whole works. This varies from person to person as a lot of it is up to your ambition and spare time.

The bigger your intended budget, the more hassle involved in trying to achieve this goal. It is not a pleasant ride. It can be a frustrating catalogue of meetings with sympathetic individuals who smile at the right times, but keep their purse strings closed. Everyone wants to get funding, you will not be the only one out there. It is a small network of 'industry professionals', who once in a while get wheeled out to meet the 'peasants', or will invite you for a meeting and give encouraging words. At the end of the day, no one is going to pour money into a project that is being undertaken by individuals with no track record. It is a really tough club to break into. You might go mad in the attempt.

If you pester people enough, a few doors may open. You may even just want to call up a big broadcaster and ask to speak to someone from the drama or comedy department – audacity and ingenuity remember – to see if you can come in for a chat or at least pick their brains in some way. They are usually quite eager to speak to new talent once they find out that you are not another desperate actor trying to get lucky. Although this may seem a very long-winded way of doing things (and it is), it's what a lot of people before you have done. Some have been lucky and others have not. But it's a vital first step into the world of networking as this is the way in which you can enter a world that may allow your film to be made.

From this first meeting, or telephone conversation with someone who's in the industry, you may come away with a few names and numbers which may in turn result in a few more names and meetings which all help on the quest to get your film made. This is networking, it is how the industry works, and it is what I had to do a few times to get a few jobs as well as get things moving with my first film. Basically, if no one knows you exist and that you are carrying a film script around then there's no way you are going to get very far.

Many directors of dramas, documentaries and feature films got their foot on the ladder by just introducing themselves to some relevant people when they were all young guns. It is how the film and television industry works.

Getting the money together to make your film may be one of the most complicated and confusing odysseys you will ever experience. Back in 2000 there was a brilliant series on Channel 4 in the UK called *Movie Virgins* on this exact subject – all about the exploits of two first-time film makers – that serves to show the two basic methods of getting your film completed.

DIY versus studio backing

One film maker was hawking his script about, networking everywhere and anywhere with industry professionals while the other was doing whatever he could via his own methods and efforts. If you ever get a chance to see this brilliant documentary then all of the above and other parts of this book will make amazingly clear sense.

The two examples of film-making levels on which the documentary series focused were a great illustration of how films are made (and try to be made) every year. The low-budget guy was getting deals on costumes, cameras, film stock, lights, even a cameraman, and he was doing things as and when his meagre resources allowed. There were long gaps in the filming and editing due to the fact that there was no equipment or resources to film with on that day, or he had been kicked out of the edit suite in preference to a paying customer. It was painful watching him go through all this agony in the name of his dream and I had total sympathy for him. In the end his persistence and luck paid off and I'm happy to say he pulled it off.

In contrast, the guy hawking his script around was going through similar agonies – except he didn't have one foot of film to show for it all. He called up every studio, went to Cannes to network, you name it he did it. He even hired a studio so he could screen test a couple of potential actors and actresses. Through the tonnes of stress and desolation, finally he was able to clinch a film deal and go ahead with his production with all the plush resources of the studio backing him.

Two ways to make a film – both incredibly hard to accomplish.

Assessing your resources

Congratulations! You've got some money. Now the question you must ask yourself is this: is it enough to make the film? If the answer is 'no', then you must either:

a re-budget your film, or
b try to get some more.

To re-budget your film, you have basically got to make do with what you have, and this may not always be practical. However, remember that you may be chasing a dream when you think that you don't have enough money. Don't go killing yourself in an agonizing attempt to get more money. It may be that the resources and money you already have in your possession are more than enough to get your film made with a little ingenuity and improvisation. What you have may be all you need to make your film.

However, if this is not the case, then you have to take a long and critical look at what the proposed budget for your film is, break it down into individual costs – as per the section on costing – and see what things you can do without. If you truly, honestly, no-way-about-it feel that you need more, then you must try to get it. Now this probably has some of you groaning in anticipation at the thought of going through the rigmarole of fund raising again, but take note, when you have been given some money, people and organizations will take you quite seriously. The thinking behind this is: 'If they've been given money, then *maybe* we should'.

The process of accretion is quite fundamental to fund raising; the theory being similar to rolling a pebble down a snow-covered mountain and it turning into a huge ball of snow by the time it reaches the bottom (although sometimes the pebble gets stuck). With the money you've been given, it will definitely be worth contacting the aforementioned funding bodies again.

They'll probably remember you, but this time you've got a wad of money that you want them to match.

Match funding is a tit-for-tat exercise in money raising. Someone gives you some money, then someone else gives you an equal amount, then with that money you go somewhere else and get some more, and so on... Do bear in mind though, that it is not always as 'text book' as it appears. It takes lots of telephone calls, letters, faxes, meetings, stress, anger and waiting. Even then you still might get nowhere.

Try to create and maintain a confidence in your project and yourself as a film maker. As mentioned in the first chapter, things will not always go your way. Be prepared for disappointing turnouts and let downs and then think of a way around these obstacles. Making a film is not something that everyone can cope with mentally. It's not just a hobby or a pastime, it's an obsession, and unless you adopt this obsessional way of thinking you may not get very far.

Bottom-line rules of funding

- Think long and hard about the scale of your film. Just because you're making a film doesn't mean you need to start worrying about large amounts of cash, completion bonds and numbered accounts in Switzerland.
- Keep reviewing your resources as you may find you can start making your film long before you originally planned to do so.

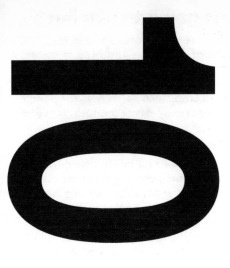

10

fine-tuning your vision

In this chapter you will learn:
- the importance of planning and/or storyboarding your film
- the basic rules of filming and presenting your actors
- how to translate script into moving images.

How on earth am I going to film this?

Imagine for a moment that you are very knowledgeable, qualified and competent in all aspects of operating any camera system under the sun. You also have all the related pieces of equipment and kit that will allow you to achieve any camera effect. Now here's a task for you. There is a large, lush oak tree in the middle of a field and it's a calm, bright, sunny day. Your task is to film the tree for 30 seconds.

Look over the situation again and then really think hard about what you will do. Some of you may feel a bit mystified by this; others might already be erupting with vivid and fantastic ways to make filming the tree look very interesting and 'art house'. You see, when you're a film maker it's your role to tell a story in a primarily *visual* way. You've got to make things interesting to look at. If your solution to the above situation was to film it straight on for 30 seconds, then you seriously need to rethink your visual approach.

However, it is worth mentioning that a certain Andy Warhol filmed the Empire State Building for eight hours from the same viewpoint. Although this piece of film is highly regarded by aficionados in the art world, it is hardly the kind of thing that had people queuing up at the cinema so they could sit on the edge of their seats.

Storyboards

One of the elements that fine-tunes the latter stages of pre-production is the storyboard. You probably all know what a storyboard is and what its function is. It's the visual instructions for the camera work of the film; it's how the shots of the various scenes will be **framed**, that is, visually presented. It's a very important function of large-scale feature length films. Imagine a top Hollywood director making his way through the hoards of crew, extras, actors, actresses, equipment, props etc. and saying, 'Oh dear, I haven't really thought about how to film this scene.'

In the context of low-budget, low-scale films, the role of storyboards is very subjective – some need it, some don't. I would have liked to have had a storyboard for my first feature film, but I didn't know anyone who was prepared to draw thousands of comic-style pictures for free, so I had to give it a miss. Instead, I took a close look at every part of my script, divided it up and marked out what the camera moves, framing etc. were to be with a red pen next to the relevant text. Very simple indeed. If I had attempted to draw a storyboard myself, it would have been a confusing mess of stick people in one-dimensional rooms.

If you feel that you really need a storyboard, but are 'pencilly challenged', a great tip I picked up is to do a 3-D storyboard using Action Men, Barbie dolls or Star Wars figures etc. You can take photos, or film the various stages with a camcorder. The latter method would allow you to narrate the dialogue and choreography. For me storyboards serve two functions:

1 They can help to explain the more complex scenes of your film, such as a Kung Fu battle or chase, as well as the film's general style.
2 It shows people (for example, possible backers) what your ideas are, and that you are organized and serious about your film.

If you are a bit perturbed about how your film should look in relation to formulating some kind of provisional mental storyboard, then simply rent a load of films by your favourite directors and take a look at how they do it. Another good method for generating ideas is to read action comics or those graphic novels based on popular sci-fi films. They contain a wealth of statically framed pictures, and I personally reckon they're the best method to pick up ideas about how to present a scene as it's easier to 'pause' a comic book than a video. You also don't have to take it back the next day!

> **Helpful tip**
>
> To practise framing, look through the eyepiece of a photographic camera to see what looks hot and what doesn't. We will come back to framing later as it is a gigantic subject.

Continuity

Continuity is the basic insurance that elements of a scene remain consistent throughout. For example, making sure that people are wearing the same clothes in a scene, that their hair is styled the same way, or that the decorations on the walls don't move around. Lapses in continuity can have varying effects on a film.

In a very serious, no-laughs-allowed kind of film, continuity errors are gravely embarrassing. Imagine in *Schindler's List* if Mr Schindler entered a room wearing his trilby and then exited wearing a baseball cap? Ouch! The balance, tone and mood of a very serious and intense film could be ruined. In zany comedy films continuity errors can have the opposite effect – they can enhance the film and make things funnier. In Tim Burton's *Mars Attacks*, Jack Nicholson's character wears a variety of different ties in the same scene. Although not immediately noticeable, it does add a certain madness to things.

In general, you'll probably find that the only people who spot continuity errors are the film's director and overzealous/sad film critics. I'll cite an example. How many of you have ever spotted the fellow in the green T-shirt suddenly standing behind Chewbacca and Han Solo in the cockpit of the Millennium Falcon as they escape from Tatooine in *Star Wars*? (This is only visible in the widescreen version though.)

Continuity errors are usually the result of a set that is very busy with lots of people bumping into and unwittingly moving props, light angles etc. Also, when a scene isn't filmed in one session, or over consecutive days, the original set-up might not be fresh in people's minds. It is particularly with the latter case that actors may turn up wearing different clothes, or decorations on a desk may be rearranged or partially missing. The best way to combat this is to use a photographic camera – preferably a Polaroid. By doing this you can visually document your set/actors' clothes for the purposes of smooth continuity, so that when you return to film the scene, you can point to the photo and say, 'This is how it was last week'. Make sure you use a marker to write on the back of the Polaroid picture referencing date and scene, otherwise you could end up with a collection of photos that don't make any sense to you. Continuity just needs some basic planning and awareness to keep it in check.

Jump cuts

These gremlins usually go unnoticed when filming, but raise their ugly heads during the editing process. For example, imagine a scene where a man is walking down a street and in mid-step he's suddenly indoors in the middle of a telephone conversation. This is a jump cut.

Jump cuts can be two shots from two different locations, or one shot that has the 'middle' missing. In the latter case an example would be someone opening a door and then suddenly the door would be closed and they would be out of shot. These instances can seriously confuse the viewer. The best example of a jump cut I can think of is in the film *Poltergeist*. (Yes it can happen in big films!) There is the scene when the husband and wife are talking in the kitchen just after their daughter has been supernaturally propelled across the floor, and then suddenly they're at a neighbour's door. The viewer is left wondering what happened.

When filming, the best way to protect against jump cuts is to film cutaways (see Chapter 7). These are shots that can be stuck between takes to link them together seamlessly. One cutaway for the above example of the man walking down the street would be to film a static of a house, which could then be placed between the two other shots. This would mean that the man doesn't appear 'magically' in conversation on the phone. The viewer will assume he was walking to the house in the cutaway. Simple.

Cutaways are a very good and *essential* practice to get in the habit of when you are filming. It is another example of filming with an eye for and appreciation of what you will do when you get to the edit stage of your film. You can be filming two shots and then 'cover' yourself by filming a cutaway so that you don't get caught out when editing. You can never have enough cutaways.

It should be said, however, that jump cuts can be used successfully to compress time in the film's narrative and make things a bit weird and disorientating. Take a look at some of the frantic and energetic sequences from *Natural Born Killers* to see what I mean.

Good and bad framing

Framing is a truly enormous subject. It is essentially a subjective commodity because no two people will be inclined to film the same piece of dialogue, or the same scene or the same shot in the same way. That said, there are a few basic technical rules to take into consideration. In no particular order:

Filming people

In your film there will no doubt be dialogue. This obviously needs to be filmed but, before you film a two-minute conversation using a single mastershot, think about what you are trying to do here. What you are doing is visually illustrating that two people are interacting. No big revelation. However, within that simple statement is the driving force of your framing: you have two people, who will, perhaps, be sitting opposite each other, so one will be on the left and one will be on the right. It's very important to remember the last bit: *one will be on the left and one will be on the right.* If you get this simple equation mixed up your scene will look terrible.

So, with the basic mastershot there is Actor A on the left and Actor B on the right (see Figure 9).

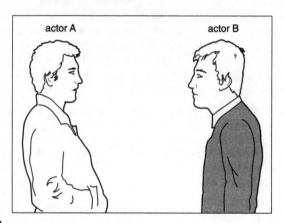

figure 9

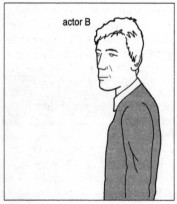

figure 10

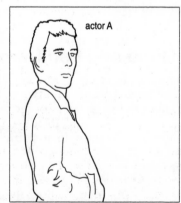

figure 11

In the cutaway of Actor B, the face is looking to the left (see Figure 10). In the cutaway of Actor A the face is looking right (see Figure 11). Thus, in the edited scene the actors will be facing their respective directions all the way through the scene. What I'm saying here is: *Don't cross the line*. This expression is a basic framing rule. If you can imagine the above filming set-up from overhead, and if you were to draw a line between the two actors, then the camera will always stay on one side of the line otherwise people will start to look as if they keep spontaneously changing direction (see Figure 12).

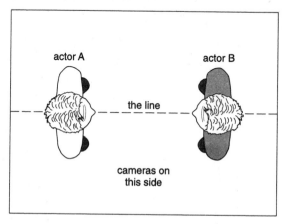

figure 12

The best example of this rule is television coverage of a football match. Team A has the goal on the left and Team B has the goal on the right. The cameras are always on one side of the pitch. Imagine if a camera was filming a footballer running with the ball and then it cut to a different camera view from the other side of the pitch. It would appear as though the footballer had instantly started running in the opposite direction. This is why, during football matches, the cameras will usually only ever cross the line if they have got better coverage of a goal or corner kick and then there is normally a sign or note made that they are using a view from the other side of the pitch.

Even if you are filming a few people it is very important to ascertain where the line is. It may be between two points in a room, for example. Ignore this line at your peril, unless, of course, you wish to make the situation look manic and surreal. Crossing the line is often used during interrogation scenes to illustrate confusion and put a 'twist' on the passing of time.

With these pointers in mind, it is important not to lose track of the basic need to present your subject in an agreeable way. This basic framing (as opposed to sequences which we will look at later) is the way your subject – a building, person or object – is presented. The way it is done can have very strong effects on the film's narrative and visual style. Imagine you are filming a woman speaking into the camera lens. If she was in the centre of the frame then the viewer's attention would be totally on her (see Figure 13). Now if only her head, from the eyes up, were visible in the bottom left corner of the frame then she would look very inferior and insignificant (see Figure 14).

Also, when an actor is speaking to someone in a scene you must frame accordingly. For example, if you have a side view of someone speaking to someone out of shot (not visible) to the left, a good way to frame it would be to have the subject (the actor) towards the right of the frame, facing the space to their left (see Figure 15).

If you did this shot with the actor 'crushed' against the left of the frame with a large gap behind him, then the effect would be very odd. It might also suggest to the audience that something will jump on the actor from the space behind him (see Figure 16). Don't believe me? Then read on...

Have you ever seen a film, usually a horror or thriller, when the hero has just run away from some monster or baddie and they've come to rest in a long corridor or alleyway? Ever noticed how the panting hero is usually in the left or right foreground while the entire length of the corridor/alleyway is visible behind them? (See Figure 17.) It makes the audience think that something's going to come down and get them doesn't it? However, just as with continuity, unorthodox framing could be the way to present *your* film in the way *you* want.

Rules aside, framing can give your film a certain style. By carefully considering what shots to use you can add a bit of weight and power that will complement the script and help tell the story. For example consider the old gem on page 116:

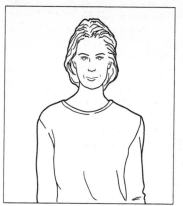

figure 13

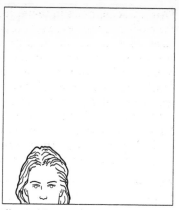

figure 14

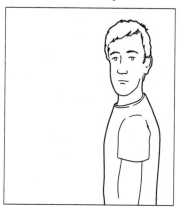

figure 15

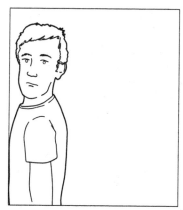

figure 16

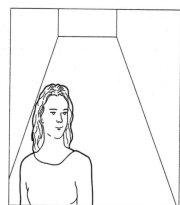

figure 17

EXT. Desert town. Empty street - Day
A cowboy walks down the deserted main road.
He stops and lights a cigarette.

Nine times out of ten what the director will do here is film a low-angle shot from the ground that shows the entire length of the road with all the shops, saloons and buildings and then one black boot will appear at the edge of the frame. So, if the road goes off and to the right of the frame, the foot will appear in the bottom left of the frame (see Figure 18).

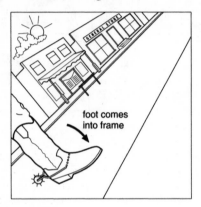

foot comes into frame

figure 18

You must have seen a film like this. What a shot like this does is tell the audience that the foot (that is, the cowboy) means business. He is a powerful individual and he has just arrived – really arrived!

Now imagine if the framing had been different. For example, the shot has been the town from a distance and walking towards it, in the middle ground, is a black-clad figure. It just wouldn't have the same gravity to it. The latter shot would just say to an audience that someone is going towards the town – it is a completely different shot, which 'tells' the audience something else.

Not stopping here, how would you continue the scene using interesting framing? There are quite a few possibilities. Since we are trying to establish the fact that this cowboy character is rather mean, how about placing the camera in front of him, low to the ground, facing upwards and walking in front of him? (See Figure 19.) The effect of this would be that the cowboy would look like

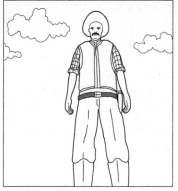

figure 19

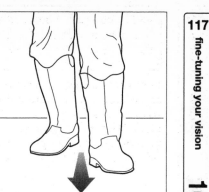

figure 20

a giant, so reiterating the power he is supposed to have. However, one drawback with this framed shot is that any suspense you might be trying to build up would instantly disappear, because the man's face (depending on the detail included in the shot) and entire form would have been revealed. So, how could we continue with the mystery/enigmatic figure idea? How about, again, putting the camera low down, in front and walking ahead BUT only looking at the boots? (See Figure 20.) This shot would create a bit more suspense and keep the mystery side of things going a bit longer, because once again the audience will be thinking, 'Who is this guy?'

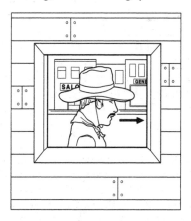

figure 21

There is so much you can do here. Next, would normally come a shot taken from inside a building looking out of the window towards the road as the cowboy passes (see Figure 21). This would suggest that the cowboy is being watched by someone as he saunters through the town. Then, to finish things off, there may be a long shot (see Figure 22), before the cowboy stops and the film cuts to a close-up of his hand striking a match (see Figure 23). The camera follows the lit match as it is raised to the end of the un-lit cigarette. Then, as the cigarette is lit, the head raises up and from under the wide brim of the hat the cowboy's face is revealed as he exhales smoke.

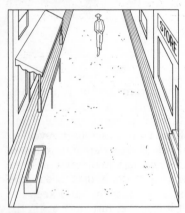

figure 22

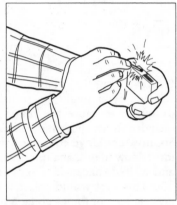

figure 23

This probably describes most cowboy films where Clint Eastwood makes his entrance. The amazing thing is that all this comes from a part of the script with no dialogue. You will need to pay attention to these 'gaps' just as much as the speaking parts. It's the simple, silent interludes that string together the scenes with dialogue in a film. Very special care has to be taken with them, otherwise your film could turn out to be very flat and dull.

Think of some more examples to help you generate other ideas. At first keep things to just four shots, for example:

> **EXT. Inner City. Busy street - Day**
> A tough-looking man walks down the street.

This character is probably a bit mean, inhabits a murky underworld and probably frightens people around him. So how would we go about this framing set-up?

- **Shot 1:** Filming through the window of a pub with a smoking ashtray and half-full pint glasses on the table as gangster walks by.
- **Shot 2:** Camera in front of gangster as he walks; close-up on cigarette coming out of mouth and then slight zoom out as he exhales.
- **Shot 3:** Long shot looking up the pavement as he walks away from the camera. People he passes timidly get out of the way and look at him as he walks by.
- **Shot 4:** Low-angle long shot on floor of alleyway with overturned bins and rubbish on the floor. Gangster walks into alley and then walks out of shot behind camera.

So, without using any dialogue – and assuming the character is suitably tough looking – we have established that this gangster inhabits a world of seedy pubs, he smokes, people are scared of him and he goes for meetings in seedy alleyways. A dangerous character has been established, all achieved by using the camera.

The cowboy and gangster examples are quite enigmatic and mean character illustrations, but not all films are like this. Not all of you will be making a cowboy or gangster movie. What about if you are making something romantic? Try this one, still keeping to just four shots:

```
INT: Large elegant living room - Night
There is a lively party going on.
A man and a woman look at each other through
the crowded room.
```

- **Shot 1:** Medium long shot of woman's face through crowded room. There is no one next to her.
- **Shot 2:** Medium close-up of man's face; he smiles as he notices something or someone.
- **Shot 3:** Camera moves towards the woman; she looks into the camera. She is slightly startled.
- **Shot 4:** Two shot: the man approaches the woman; he offers her a glass of champagne.

So from this lovely little example we can see that: the woman is on her own at a busy party; a man notices her (we presume); he moves towards her through the throng of people (simulated by the camera); he comes up to her and gives her a glass of champagne.

Again, there are other things to consider when talking about framing. So far I have just been talking about people, but what about objects and scenery? Remember in Chapter 8 when I said that your locations (and, by default, props) are your silent actors? You have got to give them some camera time, as it all adds to the colour of your film. Basically, there is no point having a great location, indoor or outdoor, if you are not going to film it. Consider this example set in a boarding school in the 1930s between a headmaster and a mischevious young pupil:

```
INT: Main corridor of Saint Cuthbert's
School - Day
Headmaster Davies hurries up to Jenkins.
                Headmaster Davies
(shouting)
  Get in my office Jenkins. And wait.
                    Jenkins
  Yes sir.
Jenkins walks into the room.
INT: Headmaster Davies's office - Day
Jenkins enters the room, closes the door
behind him and sits down on a chair in
front of the desk.
```

Right, I reckon this pupil is about to get beaten. Let's skip the dialogue and concentrate on the part from when Jenkins is sitting down. How can we put a sense of doom and fear into things using only the inanimate objects in the room and the location itself?

- **Shot 1**: Film a close-up cutaway of a photo showing Mr Davies in army attire (disciplinarian).
- **Shot 2**: Film a wide shot of the boy sitting on his own in the middle of the large room (vulnerable).
- **Shot 3**: Film a close-up cutaway of a stuffed moose's head hanging on the wall (scary).
- **Shot 4**: Film a close-up cutaway of a cane resting against the chair (the child is going to get it).

It is hoped that a certain sense of dread and overall foreboding will have been established by the framing here. Furthermore, the close-ups on those selected objects will make things a bit more intense.

All these simple details give your scenes, and overall film, the colour and life that it needs to sustain pace and, importantly, the audience's interest. The combination of the context of the scene in the script and what location and props/decorations are available, will 'tell' you what details you need to film. Listen to your silent helpers.

This, as you may be starting to see, is a HUGE subject, and one that really does not have an end. It is extremely subjective yet, at the same time, is dictated by the nature of the script and overall story. Remember that your camera is not just a box of a certain size that records images. It is a story-telling tool. It has the power to capture moving images in imaginative and delicate ways. Use it well, don't just point and shoot.

Useful tip

As a rule of thumb, think of what the scene's mastershot will be and then add detail. Soon you may have forgotten about the mastershot and dreamt up dozens of effectively well-framed shots for your scene.

Your observations of comics and watching many other films (as mentioned earlier) will no doubt make you aware of the various effects that can be created with imaginative framing.

Knowing when to stop filming a shot

When you film two people talking, the end of the conversation, and usually one of them exiting the area, will be the cue to stop filming. But what do you do when there is no dialogue and it's a shot of someone walking around a city, for example? Easy! If you are filming a long shot (a shot of something from far away) looking up a street, then when the actor walks towards the camera and simply goes past it, that's your cue.

Many people tend to make the mistake of following their subject – most commonly a person – way longer than necessary. If a person walks off, a common 'fault' is to swing the camera around to follow them and then zoom in as they walk away. This can be very awkward to watch as you can tell that things have gone on for longer than they should have.

If you are following someone with the camera, then you've got more choices of when to stop. You could follow them for a while, then stop until they walk out of shot, with the camera 'stopping' on an interesting building. Alternatively you could stop just before a corner and wait for them to walk around it. The choices are only limited by your vision – this is another enormous subject!

Knowing when to stop filming largely ties in with being aware of editing when you are filming. Don't just go filming things without an overall plan. Remember framing sequences a few pages ago? This is a great method of planning your film as a series of well thought out visual stories with considered framing, lengths of shots and so on, instead of a jumble of shots that are crudely stuck together.

Keeping track of what you have filmed

The process of filming means that the film maker (you) will end up with possibly hours and hours of filmed material. Only a smallish proportion of that will actually be used in the final edit (the *Empire Strikes Back* film crew shot 120 hours of footage). To avoid sifting through hours of out-takes, fluffed lines and other unusable stuff, keep a record when filming.

Video cameras always have **time code** displays. The format is: hours:minutes:seconds:frames (although not all domestic cameras bother with frames in their time codes). Sometimes these numbers are in the viewfinder, sometimes on a liquid crystal display on the side, or both. What this signifies is how long into the tape you are. If you are to keep track of your film, the first thing you need to do is rewind the tape in the camera and then reset the display to zero. When you've finished filming on a tape you can start logging. This is basically writing down a list of what shots go with what time code numbers, so that you end up with a list that looks a little like the one that follows.

Shot	Tape	Time code	Page of script
Richard Vincent walking up street	1	0:00:01:09	1
Richard Vincent going into building	1	0:00:03:15	1
Richard Vincent entering office	1	00:00:04:21	2
Ellie Mahonie sitting in chair in office	1	00:00:05:11	2
Richard Vincent: Dialogue **'What are you doing here?'**	1	00:00:07:13	3

With shots that relate to dialogue, it's also a good idea to mark down what the actual words are on the **log sheet** (see above), or to divide the dialogue into sections on the actual script and number them. Obviously if you have used more than one tape you will have to take this into account (the above example relates to just one tape). It also helps to label the contents of the tapes, just as you would with your music CDs at home.

Since you may have a lot of tapes and footage to log at the end of your filming, it may be a good idea to keep track of what is being filmed as it is being filmed. Logging several hours of footage can be rather dull no matter what has been filmed. If using a video recorder with an in-vision time code display, make sure that it is only visible in the viewfinder or else, for obvious reasons, it will ruin your film.

With film, you should use a clapper board, so that when you are looking through the developed film on your projector, or on video if transferred, you will see one of your friends holding a clapper that denotes:

a what the scene is
b what part of the scene it is – called a slate (the same as a shot, basically)
c which take it is.

So, for example, the clapper loader will say, 'Scene 5. Slate 13. Take 1'.

Although not as thorough as video, it does help you keep track of things during the editing process. Although you can't label film like video, you can label the film cans. However, it all gets logged when it's transferred to tape anyway (see pages 144–5).

A word of warning: When using clapper boards, try to avoid getting your fingers trapped! This happens a lot.

Other points to consider

Power sources

If you are filming indoors, then all you have to worry about is where the nearest plug socket is. If it's far away from the camera, then get an extension lead. However, if you are filming outside there will be no plug sockets available to you, so you will have to utilize the camera's battery. Always make sure it is fully charged, or your camera might suddenly die in the middle of a shot. If you have acquired a camera without its battery, then make sure you obtain a battery that has the appropriate power rating for your camera, otherwise your camera could drain it in a matter of minutes, or it might be too weak to power the camera.

Be aware of the fact that due to the increased conductivity of metal in low temperatures, batteries don't last as long in cold and freezing weather. When in a cold environment, keep them warm by wrapping them up in an old sweater or blanket.

Set controls to manual

It's all very well having a video camera that does a lot of things for you, but there will be times when this help can turn against you. The most common problem I have come up against is reliance on autofocus. An inherent problem of this feature is what I call 'a mind of its own'.

For example, when a video camera is set on autofocus, it will focus on an object in front of it – and not always on the thing you want. If the camera moves, or someone walks into shot, the camera will immediately focus on that – be it a person, a wall, a window or a light bulb! My advice is to do the focusing yourself.

This also applies to things such as the iris on your camera. If the camera has a manual iris control then use it. If you don't, you will be reliant on the camera telling you how much light it thinks it needs for the shot. If you want your shot quite dark, having a manual iris will ruin things for you by opening itself up so that the picture is as bright as possible.

Tripods

Sometimes tripods have a purpose, sometimes they don't. If you want a steady shot then you will need a tripod – no one has a hand or shoulder steadier than a tripod. Ninety per cent of all the shots you watch in a film or television production will have been filmed on a tripod. Steady shots tell the audience they are watching a film – basic but true. Steady shots can make things look very professional and make your production a bit special – because most home movies look as if they were filmed during an earthquake.

Shaky shots make a film look amateur. *However...* if you want your film to look like the television series *NYPD Blue* or *This Life*, then your tripod should be locked away for most of the filming. If you admire the shaky camera style of these programmes, then you must give careful consideration to why you want to use it and how you are going to achieve it.

This camera technique is most often used because it confers a sense of 'documentary' to what you are watching. It looks like it is *real* and not a drama. However, although the movement of the camera may appear rather chaotic, it is actually *very* choreographed. It is never a case of camera operators just turning up and filming what they want to – if this were to happen, then the results would probably be difficult to watch. During dialogue, camera operators know exactly where to point the camera, they don't just swing around blindly looking through their viewfinders every time they hear someone speak.

I know a few people who have tried to imitate this style without giving any thought to how to achieve it, and the results were painful to watch.

Holding cameras by hand, having them on shoulders, stuck on skateboards or generally moving about, can kick a bucket load of energy into your film and make it very 'real'. The best example of a hand-held camera being thrown about the place to create a 'real situation' is in the Stanley Kubrick film

Dr Strangelove, when the army is storming the air force base. The hand-held camera footage looks as though it was pinched from the street fighting in Berlin at the end of the Second World War. It's brilliant and incredibly life like. Also, more recently, the beach storming scenes during the opening sequence of *Saving Private Ryan* demonstrate how effective hand-held camera work can be.

Looking after your cameras and equipment

It goes without saying really: treat your equipment with respect and keep it close at all times. It's also worth mentioning that if you are renting a camera, give it a thorough check-up before you take it away, otherwise, the tiny scratch on the lens that was already there might translate into an extra large invoice for you when you return it.

Also, when you are filming a scene outside and you stop to take a break in the local café, take everything with you. If you don't, it won't be waiting there for you when you return! Theft of equipment is probably one of the biggest problems productions face when filming on location.

Get the best you can afford

If you intend to work on video formats, then buy the best cassettes you can afford. The better the make, the better the visual quality will be. You all know the big names, so buy them. They didn't become big names for nothing.

Film as much as possible

Again, a consideration for video users. Since video stock (tapes) is relatively cheap, it will pay to film as much as possible so that you have a good choice of camera angles, cutaways, reaction shots etc. when you come to editing.

If you are using film, then try to get it right first time, otherwise you could soon run out of film *and* money.

More on framing

Although framing has been discussed previously, there is one more aspect of this behemoth to think about: guarding against invaders. Be careful when you have framed up your shot, check it again to make sure that when you play it back at a later date you don't discover that the lead actor has a tree branch sprouting from his left ear, or that a chimney is sticking out from the top of someone's head. Pay very close attention to these saboteurs which slip into your shots and remain hidden and silent in your viewfinder. The best/worst example of this was a news report from the steps of the Museo Nazionale in Rome, Italy. In the hectic bustle to obtain a shot of the reporter amidst the chaos of what was going on, only the 'Nazi' part of the museum's title was visible next to the reporter's head. See the section on using a monitor on page 66.

Downright errors

These are things that generally compromise the look of your film. Imagine a period drama set in the seventeenth-century English countryside, with two young lovers walking down a narrow lane, when suddenly a fluorescent-clad mountain biker speeds past them. Not good! Actually, while on this subject, I am sure that a modern fibre-glass sailing dinghy merrily sails past Ben Affleck as he jumps in his car at the quayside in *Pearl Harbor*. Sad of me to notice...

Bottom-line rules of fine-tuning your vision

- First films usually fail because people are quite unaware of the power that framing can add to a film.

- Remember: the camera is a story-telling tool, so use it well.

- Don't forget to pay special attention to the basic framing when actors are talking to each other. Not giving this enough consideration can make the result very difficult to watch.

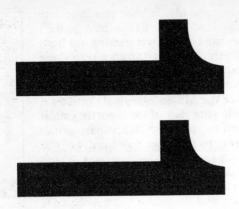

11

silence on set
...and action!

In this chapter you will learn:
- how to arrange the day's shooting
- how to avoid and guard against continuity disasters
- how to manipulate time and space by using your camera and imagination.

Time to get ready

Your actors have learnt their lines; the camera system has been chosen and rental terms agreed (if you have to pay for it); someone (preferably you) knows how to use the camera and the stock to go with it; you know where you are going to film; you've sorted out some lights; you've told everyone that you'll cover their transport and food expenses (if you've got enough cash); the costumes (if needed) have been chosen and acquired; the props have been obtained; and the money has cleared into the 'company' account (if you've applied for one). Now there's only one more thing to do – draw up the **schedule** or **call sheet**. It's all very well having everything ready to go, but does everyone know the who, where and when of it? The schedule is the timetable of filming for the entire production and will contain the following for *each* day of filming:

1 **Who is involved** Actors, actresses, camera operators, sound people, crew in general.
2 **Where it will take place** The specific address of the location with perhaps a photocopy from the local A–Z map book (if no one knows how to get there).
3 **When it will be** The exact date, along with the time it will start, and perhaps a rough stop time.

A basic template of a call sheet for a production may look something like the one overleaf.

It is a simple document that lets everyone know what is happening, although you could include additional information such as:

• Who is bringing the lights (if any are needed)?
• Who is bringing the props and costumes (if any are needed)?
• Who is bringing the sound equipment (if any separate equipment to the camera is needed)?
• Who is bringing the extension leads? (Very helpful on set.)

The type of film you are making will dictate what else is needed. With my first film a friend and I brought all of the above stuffed in the back of her Citroën, along with a few crushed actors clutching their crumpled costumes. It was all very exciting. There are few feelings as intoxicating as the anticipation of the first day's filming.

Call Sheet

Production name:

Date:

Director
Telephone number:
Mobile number:
Address:

Camera operator
Telephone number:
Mobile number:
Address:

Sound recordist
Telephone number:
Mobile number:
Address:

Actor 1
Telephone number:
Mobile number:
Address:

Actor 2
Telephone number:
Mobile number:
Address:

Actor 3
Telephone number:
Mobile number:
Address:

Meet 08:30 Little Wickton Train Station.
Drive to location: empty shop, number 10 High Street, Little Wickton.

09:00–09:30	Set up equipment
09:30–13:00	Film Scene 2
13:00–14:00	Lunch
14:00–17:00	Film Scene 5
17:00	Pack away equipment, return to Wickton Train Station.

Film it right

As I have reiterated: film with an eye to easy editing. Although the editing process is the last stage of making a film, it is very important that you are aware of the post-production side of things as this will help you film in a way that will make life easier when you come to edit.

It is a very chilling feeling to sit down in an edit suite, or in front of the television and video, to edit your masterpiece and suddenly to realize that one (or more) of your scenes just don't 'add up' the way you thought they would. The most common mistakes that reveal themselves in post-production are:

- lack of continuity
- lack of cutaways
- awkward cuts.

A film littered with the above mistakes will look as though it was made by five different directors who have never met each other. It will appear a very disjointed mish-mash of images that will be hard to watch no matter how much you like it. Continuity errors can be subtle or incredibly overt. Someone who changes their clothes and hairstyle with each shot has been the victim of a very careless director (or whoever's task it is to keep an eye on the continuity). However, there are many things on a set that, while being hard to notice, are conspiring to make your film look terrible when you get to the edit stage.

Clocks

The most common culprit is the wall clock. With all the chaos and bustle on your set, everyone will ignore the clock until it is time to edit and you notice that the time changes by 15 minutes in each shot. This is especially bad if the scene lasts only one minute. Even major films fall prey to this 'enemy'. So what safeguards can you use to ensure a clock doesn't ruin the continuity of an otherwise perfect scene?

- Don't have a clock on the set unless it is essential to the scene.
- Don't have the clock in focus – it then won't matter if the time changes by 15 minutes with each shot.
- Switch the clock off after each shot. If you have a scene where a visible clock is an essential part of the scene, then simply take the batteries out or unplug it every time you say 'cut'. Obviously with an LCD clock you will have to re-set it each time.

Candles

Candles are other objects that cause headaches and need special consideration on set. Like a clock, they will change over time: get shorter, or get shorter *and* produce huge arrested flows of dripped wax. So, if you are filming a romantic set-up, with two diners facing each other over a table with a candle, the candle will reduce in height over time. No surprise, but it is one of those things that is forgotten and can ruin your scene. Just like the clock, the candle can alter in height to the point where it can make your scene look ridiculous. Imagine if the candle dropped by two inches in one shot, then grew four inches in another. So what safeguard can you employ here?

- Use slow-burning candles (obvious really).
- Extinguish the candle after each camera run. This keeps the candle height consistent, but may fill up the set with visible candlewick smoke.

Cigarettes

Cigarettes are another pest to watch out for. Things can go totally haywire due to the fact that cigarettes change their state more quickly than clocks and candles combined. It is quite possible to see a one-minute piece of film where in the first shot the actor lights the cigarette, the next shot shows him stubbing out the cigarette and the third shot shows him smoking a full-length cigarette again – all in the space of one minute.

The advice with cigarettes is not to have your actors smoking a full one in a scene, otherwise the above will probably happen – especially if the actor is a smoker anyway and will carry on smoking between takes.

Fringes

Watch out for fringes and other manifestations of hair. With all the heat from the lights and the general troublesome work of being on set, it is only natural that an actor with a fringe, for example, will brush their hair off their brow from time to time. This will translate into radically different hair arrangements from shot to shot.

Changing scenery

Changing scenery can also cause nightmares. I don't mean chairs, curtains, furniture and other props being moved and knocked about (although that too), but other things that you will not have much control over. Imagine the following scenario:

Our pals Actor A and Actor B are filming a scene in a street with numerous parked cars. The continuity hazard here is that one of the parked cars may move off and be replaced by something else. Thus, due to camera cuts and repositioning etc., one shot may have a lime green Harley Davidson parked next to the actors, and another a dirty great truck. This is an extreme example, but you will be surprised how many things your prospective audience will notice. Even if a car moves off further down our imaginary road, someone will notice it if it is a feature of the shot.

It is amazing what gets overlooked amidst all the frantic work of filming. While you are trying to make sure that everyone is in the their positions for the next take, and that the camera is in the right position and so on, it is only natural that some apparently minor detail of the location you are filming in is ignored. But, it doesn't stop with cars.

The weather

There is also the weather to think about. Starting a scene with bright sunshine and ending with thunder and lightning may be great for a horror film, but for other scenes it could be a bit of a disaster. Even filming by some trees that get blown suddenly by gusts of wind could spoil things, especially when you remember that some scenes will be filmed in non-chronological order. So, as you go from shot to shot you will have still trees – moving trees – still trees – moving trees and so on – not forgetting the associated sound problems I told you about.

When you get to the post-production stage of your film and you discover scenes with problems like these, the only way to fix things is to film the scene again. And this may not always be possible due to resources, actors being unavailable etc.

Get it right on the day. Think ahead. Plan for everything.

Cutaways

Although cutaways were mentioned in Chapter 10, they are also brilliant safeguards for a multitude of potential problems in your films – not just for covering over jump cuts. Think of cutaways as not only an invisible yet very strong glue that will bind together the many shots that make up your film, but also points of visual detail within your story. A cutaway is a shot that reveals some detail that is not covered by the mastershot. Essentially, it is a method of bringing attention to something by changing shot, and then in edit, continuing with the scene. Cutaways serve two basic functions:

- linking up two awkward shots
- bringing attention to something.

Imagine this scenario in a script:

```
INT. Richard Vincent's office - Night
Richard Vincent is seated behind his desk.
He is sipping a small glass of whiskey and
reading the sports pages of the newspaper. As
he reads he raises his eyebrows.
```

It could be filmed as follows:

- Shot 1 – Wide shot. Richard behind his desk.
- Shot 2 – Cutaway, close-up: line from newspaper '...golf player spontaneously combusts...'.
- Shot 3 – Close-up. Richard raises his eyebrows.

So, through this shot sequence and cutaway method, we can see what is causing Richard to raise his eyebrows. If there was no Shot 2, then this scene wouldn't make any sense as the audience wouldn't know what was going on, that is, why he raised his eyebrows.

Now have a look at this example.

```
INT. Richard Vincent's office - Night
Richard Vincent is sitting behind his desk.
He is sipping a small glass of water and
reading the sports pages of the newspaper.
Somewhere in the building some glass
smashes.
He goes to investigate.
```

The following is how not to film this scene:

- Shot 1 – Richard seated behind his desk.
- Shot 2 – Richard walks into the corridor, he is holding a pistol.

Although the above may not read badly, in the context of moving images it would be a rather awkward edit. It would appear as though Richard has suddenly 'teleported' himself from Shot 1 to Shot 2, especially since in Shot 1 he is sitting still and in Shot 2 he is moving. Shots that go from stop to movement, or movement to stop need special care otherwise they will look uncomfortable when edited together. Better to do it like this:

- Shot 1 – Richard behind his desk.
- Shot 2 – Shot of exterior of building. Sound of breaking glass. Shot stays on building.
- Shot 3 – Richard emerges from a door in the front corridor, holding a pistol.

By using Shots 2 and 3 we have a more flowing narrative, the audience will have an idea of what is going on and the shots will link together better. Also, the cutaway will compress the time of the scene – during Shot 2, it will be assumed that Richard has heard the noise, got his gun and gone to open one of the doors into the main corridor. Such is the power of a good and precise cutaway. Since films do not take place in real time, cutaways are one method of shortening the length of time it would take to shoot it as real. To shoot the above in real time, you would not only have to film the shots as listed, but also Richard hearing the noise, getting out his gun, getting up from his desk, exiting his office and making his way to the main corridor door.

How about the following for a quick and easy way to compress space *and* time via a cutaway?

```
EXT. Motorway near London - Morning
A car drives away from London.
It arrives in Edinburgh.
```

To do this in real time and real space would be ridiculous – you would have a shot that lasted hours. One way around this is:

- Shot 1 – Car drives on motorway heading in the direction of sign that says 'The North'.
- Shot 2 – Wide side shot. Car drives into frame past camera and out of shot.
- Shot 3 – Car drives on motorway heading in direction of sign that says 'Welcome to Edinburgh'.

Depending on the framing used with these shots, you would have a very effective mini-sequence about travelling from London to Edinburgh. If such a sequence was filmed without Shot 2 it would give the audience a bit of a jolt as the shots would not link up very well. It could be given a bit more flavour by having a few shots of the car filmed from bridges over the motorway, or of the hands on the steering wheel, the foot on the accelerator, spinning wheels etc. – all of which would reiterate the fact that the car is travelling and moving.

Cutaways is a massive subject and could easily fill a book on its own. I therefore cannot go into too much detail here. However, take a look at your script and each page will have the potential for possibly several cutaways to be employed. Pay attention to parts of the script where it calls for a change of location or even movement within the same location (such as a character moving from one side of a room to the other). Your cutaway will act as a screen to conceal the fact that 'change' has taken place. It can be used to link shot with shot or scene with scene.

For daily examples of cutaways, I again recommend that you watch news reports. Whenever there is a news story, look out for the cutaway (they are *always* there) and consider why it was used. The most common reason for using a cutaway in this environment is to join up seamlessly two different parts of an interview with a politician, member of the public or whoever. In the middle of an interview with a farmer, for example, there will suddenly be a cutaway of the farm land. What this cutaway does is mask the fact that two different and awkward shots have just been nailed together. Most commonly, the camera operator has zoomed in or out rather quickly, or re-framed dramatically (see Figure 24).

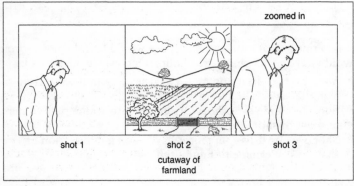

figure 24

Study news reports; they use cutaways day in, day out, and because of this the level of finesse is not as high, and therefore more noticeable, than on your favourite film.

Cutaways are a great way of linking up shots that would otherwise result in a 'jump cut', and can help you out enormously in the editing process. However, you will not always want to link up your shots and scenes using this method. There are some great ways in which you can not only change shot, but also change location and time by using some slick camera work.

Dissolves

We looked at a couple of compressed space and time cutaways above, but how about doing this with shot changes? There are a few classics that are used in every movie and television drama film. The first of these is the **dissolve**. Although the dissolve is an editing feature, it is used to brilliant effect in compressed space and time shots and scene changes. For those of you who don't know what a dissolve is, it is when two shots are joined together by means of dissolving out of one image and dissolving *into* another. Dissolves can be used to transport your audience from scene to scene. Take a look at the following script situation:

INT. Newspaper printing works - Day
The round paper rollers on the printers are spinning at high speed.

EXT. Road somewhere in a large town - Day
A car is travelling along the road.

Here is how the two shots could be placed next to each other with a dissolve.

- Shot 1: Side shot of spinning cylinder. Zoom in.
- Dissolve.
- Shot 2: Side shot of moving car wheel. Zoom out.

We have two shots of spinning/revolving objects and, when they are linked by a dissolve, the changeover will be very, very smooth. If you are using this method it helps a lot if you have objects that look similar (spinning/revolving things in this case) and if the framing is also the same, that is, the objects being filmed fill the same amount of the frame. If this is not the case, then things will look awkward despite the best efforts of your dissolve. A shot of the spinning machinery from an oblique angle and from far away would not go well with a spinning car wheel that fills the frame in a close-up.

Consider this other dissolve opportunity:

```
EXT. Forest - Day
A group of people are having a picnic and
enjoying the summer's day.
They finish and leave.
```

- Shot 1 – Group of people eating their picnic. Then tilt up to moving leaves of the trees.
- Dissolve.
- Shot 2 – Moving leaves of the trees. Then tilt down to the people packing up their picnic.

Although this example would mean filming the same set of moving and swaying tree branches and leaves, not having a dissolve would cause a jump cut, as there would be a jolt from the leaves and branches suddenly moving differently between the two shots. The dissolve would effortlessly aid the shot transition. For me, the dissolve was made for shot changes such as the ones I have just highlighted. However, remember the two shots will look smoothest if they are:

1 related – if they are of similar moving or shaped things
2 if they both fill the frame in the same way.

To confirm point 2 framed similarly – there is a dissolve in *Vanilla Sky* that goes from a back street to a hospital corridor. The framing is so precise it looks more like morphing than a dissolve.

Not obeying this guideline may result in a dissolve that is not very smooth. For example:

- Shot 1 – Man drinking in the pub while watching a football match on the television.
- Dissolve.
- Shot 2 – Leaves swaying in the breeze.

Odd, awkward even, but this may be what you, as director, want – so it isn't always a disaster. However, please note that the dissolve is not available in all methods of editing your film. If your storyboard is full of dissolves and you are using a five-year-old video cassette recorder to edit with, then you will be disappointed.

Cuts

Straightforward cuts are another way of changing shot, scene time and location in films. In fact they are *the* most popular way of changing scenes in films. So how can this be done without the use of cutaways or dissolves? Let us take the example of the picnic again, but with the one difference that the picnickers are not under trees swaying in the breeze, but are under a clear, cloudless blue sky. Look at this:

- Shot 1 – Group of people eating their picnic. Then tilt up to clear, cloudless blue sky.
- Shot 2 – Tilt down from clear, cloudless blue sky to people packing up their picnic.

When a shot cut like this is viewed, it will appear as though time has magically passed in a few seconds. Because the end of Shot 1 and the start of Shot 2 are both of exactly the same thing, it appears that there has been no shot change. The audience, therefore, has been very brilliantly fooled into thinking that nothing (i.e. the time) has changed, when in fact it has.

You may also have seen this popular compression technique in films that employ the same general method:

- Shot 1 – A man is in a hotel room. He hands a photo to another person in the room.
- Shot 2 – Close-up on the photo. Zoom out to reveal a woman holding it on a beach.

This is used in *Master and Commander* when Russell Crowe is given a model ship and then shows it to his officers. The huge advantage of this method of compressing time and space is that it relies only on you having a camera. There are many opportunities in a film to transport people through time using this camera trickery. Say, for example, you have a scene where someone is waking up, taking a shower, getting dressed and then leaving their home and you want to compress all this into a few seconds. There is a very basic method:

- Shot 1 – Shot of red wall that shows bedroom door, bathroom door and front door of a flat. There is a briefcase on the floor by the front door. A man who has obviously just got out of bed, walks out of his bedroom, closes the door and goes into the bathroom closing the door behind him.
- Shot 2 – Bathroom door opens. The man is wrapped in a towel. He opens the bedroom door closing it behind him.
- Shot 3 – Bedroom door opens. The man is fully dressed. He walks to the front door, picks up the briefcase, opens the door, exits the flat and closes the door behind him.

This is a very basic and very efficient way of doing things – albeit possibly comedic – and it can be quite effective, depending on the overall mood of the film, and what look you are trying to achieve. However, it is very important to get the shots perfect with this sort of cut. If, from shot to shot, the camera position is moved in any way, then the whole point of the exercise will be lost – the audience will know there are cuts, and very awkward ones at that. Also, if the doors are closed in one shot and open in another shot, then the effect you are trying to achieve will be ruined.

Let's try the same scenario again, but make things a bit more interesting.

- Shot 1 – Close-up of alarm clock going off. A hand switches it off.
- Shot 2 – Close-up of slippers. Man's feet go into them and walk out of shot.
- Shot 3 – Close-up of bathroom door handle. Man's hand turns handle and he opens the door and enters.
- Shot 4 – Wide shot of bathroom showing bathroom mirror. Man walks past camera, his reflection is also visible in mirror, then walks out of shot. Sound of shower running.
- Shot 5 – Medium close-up of steamed mirror. Sound of shower dies. Man's hand wipes mirror and he begins to shave.
- Shot 6 – Medium close-up of bedroom door. It opens and the man enters. He is wearing a bathrobe and towelling his hair dry. He walks out of shot.
- Shot 7 – Close-up of wall. Man enters frame from below as he straightens his tie.
- Shot 8 – Medium close-up of briefcase. Man's hand picks it up.
- Shot 9 – Long shot of front door from outside. Man opens door, exits house, closes door and walks into camera blacking out the picture.

Not only will this make for interesting viewing, but also it will mean that 15 or 20 minutes in real time have just been compressed into a ten-second sequence – all using cuts that work and flow with one another in a logical manner.

Remember: Think visually and use your imagination.

The only fundamental thing I will try to brainwash you with again, is that you should really think about your shot composition and the framing of your film, otherwise things could look very droll indeed. I know I've mentioned framing before, but it's one of those things that I can't overemphasize.

For example, say a person is standing on a street corner reading a paper. You could put the camera on the pavement and have an empty beer can in the foreground with the person in the distance so that the shot looks up the street. Alternatively, you could film the person through the traffic moving along the road, or reflected in the side mirror of a car parked near by. The choice is quite varied and will depend a lot upon your own visual style.

Watch films and critically think to yourself: 'What's the visual advantage of that particular shot?', 'What is the director trying to say?', 'Why was it done this way and not another way?' Remember: A film is a story told mostly with pictures, so make them interesting!

Another important thing to consider is to know how much you are able to do in a day. I remember my very first day directing, thinking I could get two scenes out of the way – I managed to get only about two minutes done. Don't assume that a complicated scene with several characters can be completed before lunch, otherwise half the cast might sit around twiddling their thumbs and then hear you apologetically say, 'We've run out of time.' So learn to understand what your filming pace is.

Finally, silly as it may seem, keep tabs on what you have filmed as sometimes, with all the confusion, doing things over several days and so forth, you may forget that you have already filmed a scene or certain shots. Conversely, you may think that you have filmed certain shots and scenes when in fact you haven't. Get into the habit of putting a line through the relevant parts of the script to indicate that they have been filmed.

The bottom-line rule of filming

- Get it right on the day! Don't think you can cover up any mistakes, such as bad sound or the bit where the microphone is visible. The better the quality of the recording, the better the final edit will be.

12

completing the moving 'jigsaw'

In this chapter you will learn:
- the basic points of editing
- how household technology can help you put your film together
- how to spice up your film with some music and sound effects.

Introduction to editing

Editing is not just the logical last step in the completion of your film. Nor is it the general process of sticking the various shots of your film together. Consider editing as an extension and continuation of the directing process.

When you look at the shots of your film, you will find that the emphasis of a scene may be altered radically by cutting things in certain ways, or holding a shot for a bit more or less time than planned. In other words, you can suddenly find yourself at the helm of a great narrative and aesthetic power that you never thought was there. Use this power to maximum effect.

Although you have a right to feel relaxed and happy when you've finished the actual process of filming, you shouldn't rest on your laurels for too long as you've still got the editing to do. Plunging yourself headlong into editing can be a bit of a tortuous experience. It may be an idea to have some breathing time prior to locking yourself away in the strangely addictive and secret world of editing.

When I was editing in an edit studio in Liverpool I spoke briefly to a chap from a terrestrial television station who was there editing a wildlife documentary. As he sipped his coffee, his bleary eyes met mine over the table and he said, 'I don't think any of those damned viewers at home realizes just how bloody hard editing is.' He spoke the truth. Editing a film can be like trying to do a jigsaw puzzle of a clear blue sky while wearing boxing gloves. Alternatively, it can be a breeze. No two films have the same ease or difficulty. However, the amount of pre-production work you have done should theoretically translate into a smooth edit. All those pointers and suggestions about writing the script and filming it with one eye on how it will all be stuck together, should pay off at this stage.

Having a plan in your head and, maybe, on paper of how you want it all pieced together will save immense amounts of time and stress when you are editing. It is all too easy to think of editing as something that happens when all the cameras have been packed away and all the actors have gone home, but do this at your peril! It is another process of the film production assembly line. Don't launch into this final part of the film-making process with no record of where the various shots are, no logs and with no consideration of how to bring the images and sound together.

With this in mind, what are the options open to you? There are two basic methods of editing a film – linear and non-linear.

Linear editing

This method is when you put your film together in chronological order. You play the footage from one tape and then record it using another tape in the order you choose – think of it as the visual cousin of tape-to-tape recording on a hi-fi. If you have edited your film and you want to change something, you will have to re-do everything subsequent to the alteration.

In basic terms, this system essentially consists of two rather impressive and professional-looking video players (of varying formats) connected to an **edit controller** – a good, no frills system with only a few big buttons to worry about. However, depending on make, model etc., it can be a bit limited with regards to special effects, sound channels and other technical aspects (see later). News crews in extreme locations such as jungles or deserts, use a compact linear edit system about the size of a laptop for editing their digital tapes.

The simplest linear editing can be achieved by hooking up two VCRs to a television set – giving you an instant edit suit! This apparently was how Mr Robert Rodriguez edited his legendary cheap film *El Mariachi* – remember, it's all about realizing what resources you have and using them. They might not always be apparent, so maintain your ability to think laterally. Another popular way of editing is to play the footage direct from your camera and then record it onto a VCR.

Keep it simple, otherwise you could get bogged down trying to acquire magic technology that you think will piece your film together for you.

Non-linear editing

This is carried out using digital computer technology. Using a video tape player, of whatever format, the footage is played into the computer and thus digitized into the edit system. Once the computer has digitized the footage you can play about with your film as you see fit without worrying about the problems associated with linear editing.

At the click of a mouse you can grab a shot and then stick it somewhere else within the edit in an instant. Unlike linear video editing, there are lots of buttons (you use a keyboard), a mouse and lots of options, such as special effects, sound alterations, fades, wipes etc. fitted as standard.

Computer technology had progressed to such a degree that editing this way has made its way into home computer packages and these possess features very much akin to systems used in film and television.

The days of film directors sitting in a small room with an editor sticking and cutting their films together are more or less over. The arrival of computerized digital technology has removed the need for this kind of editing.

The next time you are watching the closing credits of a film, have a look near the end where it often says: 'Originated on Eastman Color'. This means that the movie was filmed on Eastman Color – colour film made by the Eastman Company, which also manufactures Kodak film. Instead of being developed into endless reels of film, the movie went straight from the 'can' to a digital video format so that it could be digitized. The images, and then the sound, were put into the drives of a computer so that they could be manipulated for the purposes of editing.

This is the standard way of working with film these days. It goes into the camera as film stock, but via the magic of modern image-transferring technology it arrives in the edit suite in the form of a digital video tape. This is just as well as it revolutionizes the whole process, dispensing with the need to cut up little bits of film and then add sound and so forth.

The difference between linear and non-linear editing can be compared to writing an essay on a typewriter or on a word processor. They both get the job done, but the latter allows you an immense amount of flexibility and tends to be quicker and easier. One of the big selling slogans with non-linear editing technology was that it enabled you to do much more in one hour than would ever be possible on a linear system.

Non-linear editing – a practical description

OK, so non-linear computerized editing is very much the norm these days, but what exactly is it and what are the processes involved?

A good way to describe this form of editing is to again compare it with word processing an essay, only this time an essay where all the individual sentences you need are already held in the computer's memory. You then start arranging the sentences to your preference and, in some cases, shortening the sentences or altering them as they sit on the essay page. Then, when finished, you print it out. Even then, if after reading it you didn't like something, you could re-open the file and make some more changes.

Non-linear film and video editing is like that. You digitize your video or film so that it sits on your computer's hard drive, arrange it into smaller pieces and then place those smaller pieces onto something called the **time line** (the equivalent of the essay page above) to your preference. When you have finished, you record it onto a tape or burn it onto a DVD. If there is something you want to change you simply re-open the project and make your changes.

If you can word process then you can edit. All you are doing is using a mouse and keyboard to put bits of smaller files together to create one larger file, i.e. your film.

Since the majority of you reading this book will end up making your film on video formats, what are your cost-free choices?

1 Editing your film on a VCR.
2 Editing your film with a home computer software package.

Editing on a VCR

Editing your film on VCR will get the job done, but it can be rather fiddly. Basically, what you do is connect your camera to the television, through a VCR, and then record the various shots in the desired order onto a VHS tape. One immediate problem with this is a feature called **roll back** (see glossary page 169). When you press 'play' on your camera, or 'record' on your VCR, there will be a time lapse between you pressing the button and the 'play' or 'record' mechanism engaging. So, when you press 'play', it might take a second and a half for it actually to start playing the images. This, combined with the time lapse of pressing record, may mean that you record a bit of the preceding shot along with the intended one. You will therefore have to spend a considerable amount of time carefully trying to co-ordinate a smooth 'play'/'record' manoeuvre in order to get things right. Edit controllers, both linear and non-linear, allow for **frame-accurate editing**. This means you can control *exactly* where you want to start and stop the cut – with domestic VCRs you rarely have this level of precision. On a one- or two-hour film, this type of editing may well drive you mad, not to mention the fact that it's not the kind of thing you can finish in an afternoon.

Another annoying pitfall associated with linear editing is **dropout** or **degeneration** of the image. What this means is when the footage goes from the camera tape to the VHS cassette in the VCR, there will be a drop in the quality of the images and, less noticeably, the sound. Sometimes the level of dropout can be rather large – although it will have a lot to do with the quality of the tapes you have used. Editing using digital tape to digital tape tends to minimize dropout effectively, but it's still there to a lesser degree.

Editing on a computer

Editing your film on a home computer with a software package may be an option. However, computers are another 'danger point' where people can get lost in a maze of digital technology and software packages. So, some basic questions are:

- Do you have a computer?
- If you do, is it powerful enough?
- Are you prepared to get any necessary attachments, such as capture cards which allow you to sample and store clips onto your hard disk?

If the answer to any of the above is 'no', then you're probably better off leaving it, as you could soon end up in a hopeless spiral of buying packages, add-ons for those packages, then attachments for those add-ons and so on. However, many of you may be lucky enough to have such computer technology, either at home, or at college or school. If this is the case, then great.

Non-linear editing on a computer

There are lots of edit packages out there that all claim to be brilliant and swear they can turn anyone into a master editor/film director. So who to believe? The answer is all of them. The reason I say this is that it relates to what I said back in the chapter about cameras. It's not the technology that creates beauty, it's the mind and eye that use it.

People frequently ask me how great it must be to sit in front of the latest edit suite and make great films. I say, 'Yes', but then I tell them that despite the immense level of technology I've got at my disposal I still edit films in the same way the people who edited Charlie Chaplin films did.

What? By this I mean no matter how old or new a film is, it's still been edited along the same lines; cutting from shot to shot, a dissolve here, a fade there, maybe adding slow motion somewhere else etc. The principles of editing never change, only the technology. You're still doing the same things someone would have done on a Charlie Chaplin film, but you're using newer and faster equipment to do it with. That's all.

So, back to the matter at hand: what edit software to get hold of? Well, there are some that come with your computer, then there are others that you have to buy and install. Either is fine. The point is, so long as you can edit your filmed images then you're doing well. Without being too blasé, most computer editing packages are pretty similar, be it *Adobe Premier*, *Windows Movie Maker*, *Pinnacle* or whatever. The only real decider should be whether the software (and your computer) can handle all the images, sound effects and so on that you want to put through it. Another important consideration should be, 'How can I get my images *into* the computer?'

There are two main ways to get footage onto your computer's drive:

1 digitizing
2 downloading.

1. Digitizing – This is the more common method and requires you to connect your camera to the computer via a USB or **Firewire** connector. Then, via your editing software, you *capture* the footage by pressing play on your camera and recording (**capturing**) it onto your hard drive.

Now, this is all very well if you have a camera with all the leads, DV outports and cables to do this. However, what if you have something older, say a VHS or Video8 camera? Sure, these cameras will have AV (audio visual) leads just like their more modern counterparts, but such cables alone might not be enough to transfer video images into a computer. One simple and cheap option is to transfer it onto a format like MiniDV. You can just hook two cameras up using some AV cables, or go to a video transfer business as they tend to be relatively cheap. By doing this your footage can then be digitized as described above. A drawback of this option is that your footage will experience drop out, i.e. the visual and audio quality will be slightly compromised during the transfer process.

The other choice is to obtain an analog capture card or converter so that when you attach the camera's AV leads to the back of the computer it can handle and digitize the (analog) images. The disadvantage to this method is that such a card could possibly be expensive for you and mean you tearing apart your beloved computer to install it.

It is worth mentioning that digitizing tapes can be a long process as it is done in real-time. So if you have filmed ten hours of footage, it will take you ten hours to digitize it (phew!). This is the reason why professional edit suites tend have sofas and reading material in them, as well as a drinks machine (and possibly a restaurant) nearby!

Important

If you think you are going to use a computer and are ready to start digitizing your images, make sure there is a relevant port/plug/connection at the back of the computer that will take your leads. I mention this as I once arrived at the first day of editing for a colleague's low-budget film to discover that there was nowhere to plug the AV leads from the camera into the computer!

---

2. Downloading – Many of you may be familiar with this method from using digital stills cameras – the method is just the same. If you have a DVD, HDD camera, or something else that has solid-state storage, this is the method you can use. You connect your camera to the computer as per the digitizing method above and your video media (footage) goes up the wires onto your computer's hard drive.

How do the pros do it?

The pros play their footage into their edit computer by using a dedicated tape deck that is perpetually connected to their edit system instead of a camera. When tapes arrive in their edit suite they place it in the tape deck and digitize the images this way. Then, when they have finished editing, they record onto tape using the same deck.

Plusses:
• A very quick way to edit.
• Allows for a massive amount flexibility.

- Changes can be made with great ease.
- An ideal editing medium for adding music and sound effects
- Graphics can easily be incorporated into the edit, e.g. a UFO flying, a fantasy landscape or simply a gun's muzzle flash.
- Depending on where your PC is, your editing can be done from the comfort of your bedroom, office etc.
- Already configured to be compatible with modern digital cameras.
- Many editing software packages are budget priced and there is a lot of choice.

Minuses:

- Your PC may not have the memory or power to handle having large amounts of video 'fed' into it.
- The cost of upgrading for this to be possible may be expensive.
- The pro editing packages can be very pricey – comparable with buying a camera in fact.
- At the touch of a button you can accidentally delete your film (ooops!).
- A PC can crash, or get a virus, and really mess things up for you and your film.
- If you have an older camera you may have some problems digitizing your footage.

What do the pros use?

There are two main non-linear edit packages that pro film and video editors use, one is called **Final Cut Pro** and the other is **AVID**. As things stand it is AVID that is the more popular one and a great deal of what you watch at the cinema or on television will have been edited on some version of this system.

Despite the fact these two software packages are responsible for editing some pretty prestigious productions they are quite easy to use and get to grips with. In fact, if you don't believe me go to www.avid.com and download a trial version.

Sound and soundtrack

Some modern VCRs do have sockets that allow you to plug in a hi-fi for the very purpose of recording music or voice-overs onto a VHS tape. What happens here is that it only records the sound (music or voice-over) onto the tape, while still leaving the original image. Therefore, when you have edited a sequence you can then put sound onto it without having to worry about messing up the pictures in any way. However, before you start thinking about having an array of sound effects and music in your film, something to be aware of here is **sound channels**.

Every piece of sound you hear when watching a film had its own sound channel when the film was being edited. When something has been filmed and gets to the edit, the only sound will be the dialogue along with whatever the microphones recorded. This dialogue, will have a 'space' allocated for it in the edit, in other words, a sound channel. So, when it comes time to put on some sound effects there will be another channel for that and, when the music comes on, there will be another channel for that. Without this capability there would only be 'room' for one sound at a time – a piece of dialogue, therefore, may disappear under a sound effect or some background music being played over it.

The drawback when editing on an old VCR is that there will only be room for one sound at a time, so if you want to add another sound you will have to lose the dialogue for the duration of the music or sound effects. However, this does not have to be a disaster – a shot with a gun sound effect probably won't have any talking on it anyway, and music can be used for sequences when no one is talking. There are always ways around these limitations – remember, think laterally.

Some pieces of hardware do exist that can make things a bit more flexible in relation to the sound and music you want in your film, but try to avoid buying anything – there will always be someone from the local CB radio club or a friend who plays in a band who might have a sound mixer or something else you may need for the finer points of editing your film. There is always someone, somewhere, who will have a 'magic lead' that will turn your domestic VCR and television into something a bit more high tech.

Some of the aforementioned home edit software packages may have capabilities that allow you to have several different sound chanels at any one point in your film – just as their industry cousins do.

Titles, captions and text

One of the things that adds that little bit of completeness to your film is titles. It is also something that can cause a few problems for the low-budget film maker. Having great plans for a long streaming text at the end of your film may be something beyond your resources. Although some video cameras have in-built caption generators, and basic home-editing accessories allow you to compose titles, the quality is not always great. For relatively flashy looking titles and text in your film you may find this is only possible on some of the home computer edit software packages and the more professional edit systems. However, making films is all about improvisation, so what options are open to you?

One 'technology-free' method is to write your opening titles or end-of-film credits on a variety of objects and then film them. This is used a lot in mainstream films where, for example, buses move into shot with a cast member's name written in the advertising place, and then drive off, the make-up artist's name is spray-painted on the side of a derelict wall, and so on.

Another method is to write the credits on a board and simply film it. Depending on the material on which you are writing, the lettering style, lighting and camera work, it is entirely possible to achieve something very convincing.

Finally, you could film a very bright background such as a pane of glass with a very, very bright diffuse light behind it, and then stick on it cut-out black letters to form the titles or credits. The words would film as though they had been created electronically.

There are a few products on the market that can help with your editing, such as domestic edit controllers, the above-mentioned sound mixers, title machines and so on. The higher the price the more things they can do – but, as above, they can probably be borrowed from some individual or local organization after a little convincing. Please don't become obsessed with the available technology otherwise you'll end up drooling and dreaming over the 'Fungjitsu Super 1000 Home Editor' with flashing lights, shiny buttons and quadriffic sound instead of finishing your film. Remember to remain focused on your goal of making your film; don't get sucked into a confusing odyssey of edit technology. Keep it simple!

The places I mentioned earlier in this book when talking about cameras will be the same places to go to for advice and access to edit facilities. Of course, blagging will come in handy here, and by now you should be a dab hand at it. For my first film I went through my local *Yellow Pages* and got the contact details of the AVA (Audio Visual Aids) department at a local business and educational centre. After meeting up with one of the teachers and telling her what I had done, and how I really would like to use the centre's edit facilities, she allowed me to use their edit kit for free. I was able to use for absolutely nothing something that would otherwise have cost hundreds of pounds a week.

I was able to transfer the film rushes (all the takes) onto the format of their edit system, so that it could be put into its script/narrative order using their linear edit system. After a few weeks it was in my desired order but, due to the limitations of this particular edit system, I was unable to put on effects such as slow motion and widescreen. Also, due to the fact that the room I was in was a working environment (and rather small), I didn't want to cause any hassle by bringing in the cast to do voice-overs, playing in the soundtrack and sound effects etc. Therefore, I felt I had to go digital.

Digital non-linear edit services are rather expensive. If you just ring up and say you want to edit something over a week or two, then you will be quoted a price that may be enough to buy a car. You are a low-budget film maker, so do not go down this route. If you do find that you need a digital edit, just tell them what the situation is (they've probably helped out people before) and see what can be arranged. Places like this usually hire out their edit space at a very reduced rate during what is termed **down time**. This is when all the 'proper' paying customers have gone and no one else is using it. They hire out their 'fallow' space at very cheap prices. Alternatively, many colleges and universities will have these facilities and during the summer holidays very few people will be using them. So just ring up and see what can be arranged.

Hunt, scavenge and beg for your editing! To summarize the editing process:

1 Have your log sheet and go through it.
2 Based on your film, draw up an **edit script** which might look like the one shown overleaf.

Time code	Tape number	Shot	Music*	Sound effects*	Special effects*
01:11:12:04	1	Exterior of grand house	Dramatic Classical	Wind howling (loud)	Dissolve into below
00:00:12:20	2	Close-up of fireplace and zoom out and pan to Mr Vincent holding gun	Dramatic Classical	Wind howling (soft)	Dissolve from above
00:20:11:01	1	Close-up of Mr Vittorio. Dialogue 'How could you?'	Dramatic Classical	Wind howling (soft)	None
00:01:44:12	2	Mr Vincent fires gun	Dramatic Classical	Gun shot Wind howling (soft)	Flash on muzzle of gun
00:21:02:21	1	Shot of Mr Vittorio slumped in his chair	Dramatic Classical	Wind howling (soft)	None
01:32:12:06	1	Ellie Mahonie. Dialogue 'You took your time.'	Dramatic Classical	Wind howling (soft)	None

*Not all edit systems will have special effects capabilities. See section on sound channels on page 151.

Obviously an edit script is much, much longer than this and although not essential for every single bit of the film, it is a very good way of getting a rough idea of how to put your masterpiece together.

3 Edit your film.

4 Pat yourself on the back.

One pointer about editing is not to feel compelled to include a shot or scene just because you have filmed it. Even though the shot may have taken some serious aggravation to film, you may realize during editing that it just doesn't fit in with the rest of the film. If this is the case then don't include it in the edit otherwise your film could end up having some dead space in it.

Finally, many people often see computer/digital editing and then ask: 'Can I make my video look like 35 mm film?' The short answer to this question is no. The long answer is that there is a way in which you can render the images on a digital edit so that the pictures look a tad more glossy and 'filmic'. The expression that editors use is **strobing**. Without even attempting to explain the workings of digital visual technology and related hardware, this basically means that the overall quality of the images is digitally altered, so that what was filmed on a video system (commonly a broadcast format) is converted into a 'poor man's film'. This technique is very popular with some television dramas as it 'cheats' and makes things appear that bit more up-market and film like.

This way of doing things is another 'holy grail' of low-budget film makers. Since being able to actually make a film *on* film is something many dream of but few accomplish (for reasons of expense or complexity) this method is a very popular way of re-dressing the problem, so to speak – if they are able to use a digital edit system that is! However, many people can't see the logic in this: why film on a very clear and precise digital video format that gives a perfect image and then alter it so it looks different?

Those of you who end up going down the state-of-the-art digital editing route will learn that there are many things that can be done with your image, but be careful – don't turn your simple story into something crammed with various pointless edit effects. I once saw an interview with a vicar sitting in his living room turned into something that looked like Queen's Bohemian Rhapsody video.

> Use the technology, but don't let the technology use you!

When you are coming towards the latter stages of your editing, bear this quote in mind: 'A film is never finished, it is merely abandoned!' I don't remember who said the above, but it's very true. If everyone in an edit suite were to stay there until they thought the film they were working on was complete – they'd never leave. I call the obsessive editing syndrome the 'adding the salt factor'. There are so many tweaks, tucks, nips and brush-ups you can do to film when editing, it's like adding salt to soup: after a while you've ruined it.

Bottom-line rules of editing

- Be 100 per cent sure that you know where the various shots are and where the tapes are. In other words, log and number your tapes, otherwise things could become confusing.
- Don't get hung up on the fact that you're not using a state-of-the-art edit system. Putting your film together effectively is all that matters.

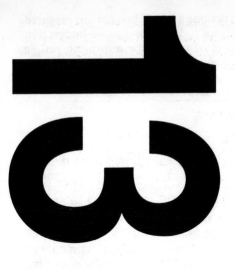

13

showing your film

In this chapter you will learn:
- some straightforward ways of exhibiting your film
- how to go about 'getting noticed'
- how not to be sued by a global entertainment company.

There is not much point in making a film if you are not prepared to show it to people. Luckily for today's low- and no-budget film maker there are a multitude of outlets for informing people about and exhibiting your visual talents. These can range from the World Wide Web or a popular monthly film magazine to blagging the screen room at a local conference centre.

Finding an outlet

Brainstorming and lateral thinking will allow you to think of places to show your film, but don't just think about getting it shown, think about getting it – and yourself – noticed. See if a few of the local film agency, film office or arts board people can come to the screening. But don't stop there. Call up a few television stations and try to get hold of someone who you think may be interested in your talents – drama, comedy or documentary – depending on the subject matter of your film. Make copies and send them off to everyone you can think of. It's all part of the process of going on to bigger things. This is how the system works.

Depending on the faith you have in your film, and your ambition, you may want to try your hand at contacting some major film and distribution companies. They may tell you to get lost, give you a large amount money to make another film or put you in contact with someone who may be able to develop another project. Look in the *Yellow Pages* or on the Internet. Just phone people and see what they say.

Copyright laws

Copyright is something that may not concern most of you. However, there may be times when covering yourself over the use of other people's images, words and music is a wise policy.

If you intend only to show your film privately, for example to friends, your local movie club or in a film class, then it will not matter if you have a soundtrack courtesy of The Beatles and film clips taken from *Apocalypse Now*. If, however, you have arranged to show it in a location where you plan to make a charge, such as a local community hall, 'art cinema' or wherever, then you could get in serious trouble. The reason for this is that you are using someone else's work (music, film, television clips) without their permission or acknowledgement, in a production that will legally be considered commercial. If you are caught you could face a massive fine that will change your hair colour.

If you are making a film that you intend to promote commercially, and you want to include 'third-party material' then my advice to you is *don't*! The cost of obtaining permission to use a song, or a film or television clip for whatever rights you require are very, very expensive – usually thousands of pounds/dollars for a few seconds.

Even if you are able to get your film on a television talent series or new film makers' showcase, they will probably first ask for documents proving that any extra material you have in your film is cleared for use by you. The same goes for Internet independent film sites.

If you want a soundtrack, then ask a friend to play their guitar, drums or keyboard to ensure you don't get into big trouble in the event of your film becoming successful. However, first make sure that the terms and conditions are agreed in writing otherwise your 'friend' may resurface in a couple of years asking for a few thousand in back-dated royalty payments.

Copyright-related matters don't stop here. For the more commercially minded, watch out if there are radios or televisions in your scenes. You may inadvertently end up with a popular song or programme in your film. The same goes for logos of brands and companies. They may not agree to 'appear' in your film and thus may sue you. Something else to consider are release and consent forms. These are forms that people sign stating that they agree to appear in your film – it's just another safeguard against future problems.

Be careful out there. Don't think that your film will go unnoticed by the company who owns the music rights to a song you are using. Many low-budget film makers have been ruined by making this assumption.

Bottom-line rules of showing your film

- Brainstorm your ideas and make copies of your film to send out to everyone you can think of.
- Be aware of copyright laws. Don't use third-party material unless you gain permission to do so.
- Make sure you get the people involved in your film to fill out release and consent forms.

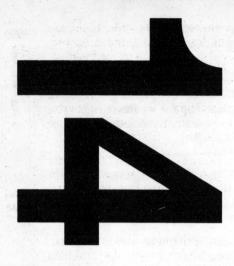

14

confessions of a film maker

In this chapter you will learn:
- what not to do
- how to avoid disaster
- how to remain in control.

Two exploded 800-watt lights, smashed bottles, spilled beer, an actress crying hysterically, a drunk lead actor, 30 moaning and bored extras and a caretaker telling me to get out of the building – not exactly how I planned on finishing my first ever day's filming. But you can never predict how these things will go.

If, at the end of your filming experience, you don't have one single amusing story, then you have been doing something *very* wrong. I hope my tales of woe/amusement will serve to highlight some of the ways not to make a film.

Obtaining sponsorship from a Czech brewery was quite a coup on a number of levels: the film had official support, the production received genuine and much-needed props, plus beer is a good way of paying cavalier and feisty actors.

Unfortunately, having about 40 people hanging around a set all day drinking alcohol can lead to circumstances that are not conducive to the making of a film. People got drunk and every so often the sound of breaking glass and a drunken expletive was heard right in the middle of a take.

Having the lead actor drink real vodka and beer for all the takes was probably not too wise either, as by the time he was on the cusp of getting the lines right – he just sighed, swooned and fell to the floor from all the alcohol he had consumed.

This was nothing in comparison to one of the other actors in the pub scenes who had also been absorbing a steady stream of vodka. By the time he had to say his lines, a stream of vomit came out of his mouth instead of the words I had written. He then passed out and had to be taken home in a wheelchair.

Adding to the festival of inebriation, a meek and mild-mannered extra drank one beer too many and turned into a psychopathic lunatic. After he had attacked a cast member and knocked over some lights, he ran out of the set and went on a crime spree in the local liquor store. I heard he was arrested later that night.

To add to my misery, one of the actresses, who was top of her drama class at college, suddenly got an attack of the nerves. Instead of walking over to the tables and serving drinks, she froze in the middle of the set and dropped a tray of alcohol on the floor. At the exact moment beer came into contact with floor, two of the 800-watt lights blew up. The caretaker of the building came in and told us to get out as he was closing up. I had not even filmed a page and a half of script. I had two scenes to get through and I wouldn't be able to hire the hall again for another two months!

Through the smell of stale beer, vomit and burning I suddenly realized how hard all this could be. Having beer flowing freely on the set was probably not a great idea, especially for actors as it seriously affected their performances. But it was all part of the learning process I suppose.

That first day was a bit of a disaster as numerous things went very wrong. Thankfully, from there on the production found its pace and the cast and crew learnt how to work together until it was a 'well-oiled machine'. The rule here is: try to keep everyone in line on set. Without a bit of order and, dare I say it, *discipline*, a large group of people can soon turn into a rabble of maniacs. Have fun, but don't let things get out of hand.

Health and safety

The general health and safety of your cast and crew should also be something to which you pay particular attention. However, no matter how diligent you are, there will always be something that goes wrong. Once, while filming an interrogation scene, we were in a long bare room with a window at the far end. I had framed the mastershot so that the entire length of the room was at an 'arty' oblique angle and tilt, and the actors and two actresses were in frame. The set-up was simple enough: the interrogation victim was between the other two actors, and I had told her to wriggle about on the bar stool on which she was tied up. Unfortunately she wriggled so much that she lost her balance, and in the process of falling off her perch knocked over a very large and heavy bronze sculpture that was on a pedestal behind her. The bronze bust then fell against the window but, amazingly, just bounced off the glass and fell harmlessly to the floor. Since this room – and window – were four storeys up, a potentially nasty accident, and possible legal headache, was averted. Luckily the actress was not harmed by the fall – and it made a great end of shot.

The rule here is: try to look at what could happen on your set that might result in someone getting hurt. Try to figure out everything so that you can avoid an accident. As mentioned earlier, wires and cables are probably the biggest potential source for accidents.

Safety is something that can be gauged through a recce, as is the overall state of the location where you want to film. Avoiding a recce may lead to unfortunate surprises...

The importance of a recce

When filming in the southern Czech Republic, I decided that it would be great if we could film something in the not-too-far away Austrian capital of Vienna. I had some 'stand-by' pages of script in the event that we made it to Austria (this was low, low budget remember). We hopped over the border and, as we all neared the beautiful and elegant eighteenth-century Schonbrunn Palace and its equally breathtaking gardens (used in a James Bond film), I was telling the cast and crew about the sheer magnificence of the place and how it was a unique location at which to film. We then turned the corner and went through the palace ground gates and I was rather upset to discover that the entire building was covered in scaffolding, sheeting and all the gardens were being dug up by JCBs and bulldozers.

Although we managed to film the scene I had written, my original shot sequence was seriously limited due to the sheer scale of renovation work going on. The rule here is: go on a recce, otherwise when you turn up for filming any number of obstacles to your film may be waiting for you.

People

Another important thing to highlight is the people factor. People – actors, crew or whoever – can hinder your film in all manner of ways. These can range from a cast member starting to get all cocky and too big for their boots just because they have been in a pantomime somewhere, to perhaps a camera operator who wants to film things in their own special way. Although many of the comments that actors and crew make can be innocent suggestions to help out a certain scene of your film, sometimes they can be a bit more awkward and meddlesome. A common one is actors improvising a tad too much or adding new lines in the middle of filming a scene. Sometimes these things can really change the focus of a scene and dilute the film from what you want it to be.

Remember: you are the boss of this project, it's your idea, you're the creator, make something that *you* are happy with. It's all too easy sometimes to agree to the energetic and show-off tendencies of a cast member, or the lighting person or whoever, in the interests of diplomacy and getting the film made. However, there may be a point when you will realize that they are going a bit too far and it does not fit in with your idea of how the shot should look, how the dialogue should sound and so on.

Know where the line is, and make sure people don't cross it. It's a tricky problem and I hope not all of you will experience it – but it can happen. It is very important to nip this one in the bud before you end up with a film that you are not happy with. The rule here is: it's *your* film; make sure it is made that way.

Another people factor is to make sure people are happy when being filmed. Some actors, while great at delivering lines, can suddenly freeze when they see a camera on them. They may even say their lines and from time to time look into the camera. Do try to avoid situations like this. You may find out that although someone is a very talented actor, they become extremely conscious when filmed, and it may take a bit of time to get over this slight difficulty (see Chapter 3).

Also, if you are out filming in the street or in another public place, it is very annoying when passing people shout and wave into the camera or suddenly get embarrassed and deliberately look away. So bear this in mind. People react in strange ways when they see a camera. I've been held up shooting a scene due to some passing lunatics offering to strip off in front of the camera.

While on this subject, there was a Greek film company in the 1970s and early 1980s that constantly made big-budget films about glamorous women who became mixed up in international espionage. In every single film there were several scenes where the heroine was seen running through the crowded streets of Athens or wherever. In these scenes you could always see people in the street smiling and pointing at the camera as they ambled on by eating a sandwich or drinking a beer. It was ridiculous to see the actress looking all forlorn when next to her was a group of locals pulling faces and giving the thumbs-up sign to the camera.

I also had an interesting situation in a hotel in Prague: after all the cast and crew had settled into their rooms on the first night, a Russian woman who was also staying in the hotel and who spoke very little English, got talking to us in the lounge and asked us what we were doing in Prague. After a while I suddenly decided to improvise a scene in which one of the characters meets up with a lady of the night as a follow-on from a scene we had filmed back in Merseyside (low budget is about capitalizing on available resources, remember). So I explained to the Russian woman what we wanted to do. She agreed to take part and so we went ahead. The scene was simple enough: one of the actors and the Russian woman walked down a corridor, into an open doorway and out again, and that was that – or so I thought. Later that evening as everyone was going to bed, the Russian woman came up to me and stated that she had not realized what we wanted her to do due to her poor English, and that if anyone saw this film in Russia then people could get killed, so would we please destroy the footage of her!

The rule here is: if you have any 'tertiary actors' make sure they agree to be filmed. Some people can be very vocal about not wanting to be filmed and you must respect their feelings. For film and television there are 'release and consent' forms that people have to sign that state they agree to be filmed – something to think about (see Chapter 13). Try to balance fun with responsibility and you won't go far wrong.

Closing thoughts

I hope this book has entertained as well as informed and that you have a good idea of what is involved in making a film.

> 'There are now more ways for more people to show *other* people how bad they are at making films.' – Director Terry Gilliam on the downside to the proliferation of digital film-making technology.

In the time it has taken you to read this book there has probably been some other piece of technology or computerization invented that means it is a bit easier, and even more accessible, to make a film. A low-budget film maker ten years ago could not have dreamt up some of the things that are now sold on every high street. However, do remember that despite all the technology and gadgets out there, making a film is about harnessing your creativity and translating this into a story of moving images. No amount of gadgetry can do this for you, it's got to come from within.

There are two kinds of people in this world: those who talk about doing things and those who *do* things. Those in the latter category make films. But remember, the best anyone can do is try...

Get out there and make your film happen!
Good luck.

glossary

ambient sound   Background sound that is picked up by the microphone in addition to dialogue etc.

aperture   Opening which controls the amount of light that eventually hits the film or video. Its size can be altered to vary the amount of light coming through.

boom   A 'pole' with a microphone on the end that allows the sound recordist to get the microphone close to the actors without appearing in shot (most of the time).

call sheet   Simple document showing the arrangements for a day's filming.

close-up   A shot that will make the subject, for example a face, fill the screen.

crash zoom   A very rapid zoom; see separate entries on **zoom-in** and **zoom-out**. Very dramatic, for example, if done repeatedly on a knife sticking out of someone's head.

There are scenes in Bruce Lee films where all the fighters are sizing each other up. The camera crash zooms in on all of them one by one. However, one problem with a crash zoom is that because the zoom is so quick, the camera operator doesn't have time to make sure that the subject ends up in the middle of the frame (sometimes only half the head is showing), thus the camera has to humbly move a bit to put things right. It happens a lot in spaghetti westerns as well.

cut   The instant when one shot joins another in the editing process.

cutaway   A shot that reveals some detail that is not filmed via the mastershot, yet has relevance to the scene. For example, two men are in a room, one is seated at a desk, the other is standing in front of the desk opening a drawer. A possible cutaway could be a close-up on the desk drawer being opened to get out a gun. In a busy pub, with two people speaking at the bar, a possible cutaway might be of some of the other people seated around the pub having a drink.

dissolve   An edit effect in which two shots are joined by means of fading out of one shot while simultaneously fading into the next.

down time   'Off-peak' times when it is usually possible to hire edit facilities very cheaply.

dropout or degeneration (of image)   The reduction in the quality of the image and sound as it is copied from tape to tape.

edit controller   Machine of varying size and complexity which links a player, or video camera, to a recorder for the purposes of assembling and editing shots together.

edit script   An idea of the intended chronology of the footage, and any effects and soundtrack etc, written out in the form of a plan. Sometimes it is only used as a guide. Also known as a 'paper edit'.

external microphone   A microphone that is plugged into the camera.

fade   A method used, either via the aperture controls (see **aperture**) or in editing, where the image fades from or fades into black. The former might be done with a countryside scene to signify daybreak, while the latter might be done as a character's eye view to indicate falling asleep or dying.

field of vision   The 'visual area' your camera will record and film at any one time.

frame   The filmed shot.

frame-accurate editing   Editing that allows editors to stop and start cuts exactly where they want.

gag   A method, and object, for reducing the amount of wind sound a microphone picks up.

gel   Coloured transparent plastic 'paper' that can be put in front of lights to change their colour, or in front of windows to maintain the white balance (see below) of the picture.

hook   The feature of your script or story that gets people interested.

jump cut   A cut in which some of the action disappears and will cause a jolt in continuity.

key light   The main light on a set, which lights everything up. Other lights may be used to film cutaways etc.

linear editing   Editing using a tape-to-tape method where the film is edited in the order in which it will be viewed.

long shot   A shot taken a long way away from the subject or building etc.

low-angle shot   A shot made when the camera is placed low to the ground facing upwards. This is very effective in making someone look domineering or huge. The opposite, having the camera high up and facing the ground, will make someone look very puny or insignificant. Remember the scene in *Oliver*, when Twist says, 'Please sir, can I have some more?' to Harry Secombe? Harry Secombe is filmed in a low-angle shot, while Oliver Twist is filmed in a high-angle shot.

mastershot   The main shot of a scene, filmed continuously with the same camera. Extras such as cutaways and close-ups etc. are filmed later and then put in via the editing process. Some film scenes are simply mastershots with nothing else, but this can be boring for the viewer.

matching   Funding process where funds are received to equal and match those you already have.

non-linear editing   A flexible form of editing where shots can be edited in a manner that does not conform to, or affect, the planned story order.

overexposure   When too much light has got onto the film or video during the filming process. This has the effect of making people's faces, and other reflective surfaces, look exceptionally shiny and radioactive. In film and television it is commonly called 'flare' or 'bleach'. It is usually caused by the sun coming out from behind the clouds, having lights that are too bright or having the aperture/iris of the camera too wide open. Overexposure is a good and popular way to film flash-back or dream sequences in a film.

pan   Moving the camera around horizontally on a tripod or shoulder for the purposes of filming someone walking, a car driving, a dog running past the camera etc.

partners   A person, or persons, with whom you may be required to form an organization or group, for the purposes of obtaining funding.

plug-in microphone   Another term for an **external microphone** (see separate entry).

reaction shot   A shot showing someone's reaction to something in the action. For example, a wife is speaking to her husband. The wife says, 'I used to be a man.' There would then be a reaction shot of the man's face (usually in close-up), filmed as cutaway.

recce   Short for reconnaissance. Having a look at a potential location.

redhead   Popular professionally used light

reflectors   A hand-held object made of reflective material which is used to increase the light illuminating a subject.

reverse cut   This is when something has been filmed from two opposite angles. If someone is walking it will give the effect that the person has suddenly changed direction. However, it has its use: if two people are sitting at a bar, there may be a reverse-angle cut to show the view from behind the bar.

roll back   A mechanical feature of a video camera or VCR. When 'record' or 'stop' is pressed, the tape can physically roll back slightly which means it has not stopped at the intended place. With a video camera this can mean the few final moments of a take can be *clipped* when the record is stopped then started again. When using a video camera, always keep it recording for a few seconds after you have finished recording your subject. When editing with a VCR it can mean that a few moments at the end of a shot can be recorded over.

third-party material   Material, such as music, film clips or text used but not owned by the film maker.

scenic projection   You've all seen this in films, usually employed when someone is driving in a car and you can the see the road going behind them at impossible speeds and turns. A film or slide projector is used to project an image onto a screen while the actors perform in the foreground. Make sure, however, that the projector is *between* the actors and the projection surface, or behind it, otherwise the results will look awful! Watch the film *Natural Born Killers* to see how effective scenic projection can be in a contemporary film.

set The place where you film a scene. Can be decorated to the guidelines in the script, such as a room, or left as it is, a city for example.

schedule Another name for the **call sheet** (see separate entry).

shot Something that is filmed in one continuous run of the camera, i.e. between the director saying 'Action!' and 'Cut!'.

sound channels 'Spaces' allocated via an edit system, and then in turn onto the film, for each different type of sound, e.g. dialogue, sound effects, music.

strobing Digital editing method in which images sourced on a video format are altered to appear more 'film looking' in texture.

time code Numeric display in a camera viewfinder, or tape player, used to reference where shots are.

tilt Like pan (see separate entry) but in a vertical direction, for example, to tilt down the height of a tall building.

treatment A concise synopsis of the intended film script outlining its story and characters. Usually on no more than one A4 piece of paper.

two shot A shot where two people are shown dominating the frame.

underexposure The opposite of **overexposure**. Caused by the sun suddenly going behind clouds, having the aperture iris closed too much or by using ineffective lighting. Underexposure can be a good way of simulating twilight or night.

whip pan Like a **pan** but much faster. So fast in fact that the images are all blurred. A very popular method of jumping from scene to scene in television spy spoof/super hero series of the 1960s – usually accompanied by some equally rapid bongo drumming.

wild track Recording of the natural sound of a location to use as a background track in the edit.

zoom-in Makes the subject progressively larger in the frame.

zoom-out Makes the subject progressively smaller in the frame.

taking it further

Useful contacts

Some useful addresses

Here are the contact details of some groups and organizations in the UK. The list starts off with the regional arts boards, which are often the first calling point for aspiring film makers.

The Regional Arts Councils

Arts Council of Northern Ireland
MacNiece House
77 Malone Road
Belfast BT9 6AQ
Tel: 028 90 385 200
Fax: 028 90 661 715
Website: www.artscouncil-ni.org

Arts Council of Wales
(Cardiff Office)
9 Museum Place
Cardiff CF1 3NX
Tel: 029 20 376 500
Fax: 029 20 221 447
Website: www.artswales.org.uk

(Colwyn Bay Office)
36 Prince's Drive
Colwyn Bay LL29 8LA
Tel: 01492 533 440
Fax: 01492 533 677
Website: www.artswales.org.uk

(Camarthen Office)
6 Gardd Llyadaw
Camarthen SA31 1QD
Tel: 01267 234 248
Fax: 01267 233 084
Website: www.artswales.org.uk

Arts Council England, East
Eden House
48–49 Bateman Street
Cambridge CB2 1LR
Tel: 0845 300 6200
Fax: 0870 242 1271
Textphone: 01223 306893
Website: www.artscouncil.org.uk

Arts Council England, East Midlands
St Nicholas Court
25–27 Castle Gate
Nottingham NG1 7AR
Tel: 0845 300 6200
Fax: 0115 950 2467
Website: www.artscouncil.org.uk

Arts Council England, London
14 Great Peter Street
London SW1P 3NQ
Tel: 0845 300 6200
Website: www.artscouncil.org.uk

**Arts Council England,
North East**
Central Square
Forth Street
Newcastle upon Tyne NE1 3PJ
Tel: 0845 300 6200
Fax: 0191 230 1020
Textphone: 0191 255 8500
Website: www.artscouncil.org.uk

**Arts Council England,
North West**
Manchester House
22 Bridge Street
Manchester M3 3AB
Tel: 0845 300 6200
Fax: 0161 834 6969
Website: www.artscouncil.org.uk

Scottish Arts Council
12 Manor Place
Edinburgh EH3 7DD
Tel: 0131 266 6051
Fax: 0131 255 9833
Website: www.artscouncil.org.uk

**Arts Council England,
South East**
Sovereign House
Church Street
Brighton BN1 1RA
Tel: 0845 300 6200
Fax: 0870 242 1257
Textphone: 01273 710659
Website: www.artscouncil.org.uk

**Arts Council England,
South West**
Senate Court
Southernhay Gardens
Exeter EX1 1UG
Tel: 0845 300 6200
Fax: 01392 229 229
Website: www.artscouncil.org.uk

**Arts Council England,
West Midlands**
82 Granville Street
Birmingham B1 2LH
Tel: 0845 300 6200
Fax: 0121 643 7239
Website: www.artscouncil.org.uk

**Arts Council England,
Yorkshire**
21 Bond Street
Dewsbury
West Yorkshire WF13 1AX
Tel: 0845 300 6200
Fax: 01924 466 522
Website: www.artscouncil.org.uk

National organizations

The British Academy of Film and Television Arts (BAFTA)
195 Piccadilly
London W1V 0LN
Tel: 020 7734 0022
Fax: 020 7734 1792
Website: www.bafta.org

BAFTA have central offices in London, but they have regional centres around the UK. They can offer advice and a wide range of support to film makers.

The British Film Institute (BFI)
21 Stephen Street
London WIT 1LN
Tel: 020 7255 1444
Website: www.bfi.org.uk

The BFI exists to promote and help the production of films in the UK. Although it has a limited funding capacity and runs a few schemes from time to time, it mostly advises and acts as a resource for film-making information, be it other organizations or individuals, who may be able to help you.

The Film Council
10 Little Portland Street
London W1W 7JG
Tel: 020 7861 7861
Website: www.filmcouncil.org.uk

A national organization that promotes, supports and encourages the UK film industry. It provides grants and funding for film makers, but be warned – it tends to concentrate this help only towards larger 'professional' films. However, like many other places there may be someone there who can help you.

Pro8mm (USA)
2805 W. Magnolia Blvd
Burbank
CA 91505
USA
Tel: 818 848 5522
Email: sales@pro8mm.com
Website: www.pro8mm.com
(both USA and UK/Europe)

Pro8mm (UK & Europe)
Grafton House
Suite 14
213 Golden Square
London W1F 9HR
England, UK
Tel: 020 7439 7008
Email:
Europe@pro8mm.com

This company (as the name suggests) specializes in services, cameras, film and accessories to do with 8 mm film. They are used by professionals and amateurs alike and also deal with 16 mm film. A great place to start if you want to look into this format of film a bit more closely.

A general description of some other arts and funding bodies around the world:

Finding funding (and information) to help make your film is something that is never too far away no matter where you live. Arts Boards are not only regional organizations in the UK, but they exist in other countries. For example, around the world there is Americans for the Arts, The Australian Council for the Arts and The Canada Council for the Arts to name only three.

With regard to Charitable Trusts (or Philanthropic Societies as they are sometimes known), these exist around the globe and there is always a publication, be it an almanac or directory, that lists them for a particular country. Likewise, every major town around the world will have some manifestation of community film and video. In many cases they co-exist with commercial companies. In addition to having bursaries available, they also often run training days in the use of film- and video-making equipment. Just like community film and video organizations, there are film agencies all over the world for most major towns and national districts. Even if you don't know it, there is probably one in your area.

Lotteries around the world vary a great deal in terms of the way they are organized and what they do with the revenue they make. Some may have a percentage that they pay into charities or other organizations. For example, the Lotteries Commission of Western Australia pays money to the Western Australia Film Industry as well as other arts bodies. However, some of you may be in a part of the world where the lottery has no provision for film or arts and money is given to education or health programmes instead.

Below is a list of bodies in Australia, Canada and the United States of America which you may find useful.

Australian Council for the Arts

Street Address:
372 Elizabeth Street
Surry Hills
NSW 2010

Postal Address:
PO Box 788
Strawberry Hills
NSW 2012
Australian Business Number: 38 392 626 187
Tel: (02) 9215 9000
Fax: (02) 9215 9111
Toll Free: 1800 266 912
Email: mail@ozco.gov.au
Website: www.ozco.gov.au

Australian Film Commission

Postal Addresses	Street Addresses
GPO Box 3984 Sydney NWS 2001	Level 4 150 William Street Wooloomooloo NSW 2011 Tel: 61–2 9321 6444 Fax: 61–2 9357 3737 Toll Free: 1800 226 615 Email: info@afc.gov.au
PO Box 404 South Melbourne Victoria 3205	Level 2 120 Clarendon Street Southbank Victoria 3205 Tel: 61–3 8646 4300 Fax: 61–3 9696 1476 Toll Free: 1800 338 430 Email: infomelb@afc.gov.au

Pacific Film and Television Commission

PO Box 94 Albert Street Brisbane Queensland 4002	Level 15 111 George Street Brisbane Queensland 4000 Australian Business Number: 57 859 074 040 Tel: 61–7 3224 4114 Fax: 61–7 3224 6717 Email: ojohnston@pftc.com.au Website: www.afc.gov.au

Americans for the Arts

Washington Office	New York Office
1000 Vermont Avenue NW	One East 53rd Street
12th Floor	New York
Washington DC 20005	NY 10022
Tel: 202 371 2830	Tel: 212 223 2787
Fax: 202 371 0424	Fax: 212 980 4857
Website: www.artsusa.org	

The Canada Council for the Arts

350 Alberta Street
PO Box 1047
Ottawa
Ontario
K1P 5V8
Tel: (613) 566 4414
Fax: (613) 566 4390
Toll Free: 1 800 263 5588
Website: www.canadacouncil.ca

National Film Board of Canada

Head Office
Constitution Square
360 Albert Street
Suite 1560
Ottawa
Ontario
K1A 0M9
Tel: (613) 992 3615

Operational Headquarters

Norman-McLaren Building
3155 Cote-de-Liesse Road
Saint-Laurent
Quebec
H4N 2N4
Tel: (514) 283 9000
Toll Free: 1 800 267 7710

Postal Address
Postal Box 6100
Centre-ville Station
Montreal
Quebec
H3C 3H5
Website: www.nfb.ca

Websites

www.nextwavefilms.com
US-based website with some very helpful, revealing and detailed examples of how current Hollywood directors started out and how they achieved top results by using many of the methods highlighted in this book. Also has excellent links to film-making equipment, funding avenues and distribution.

www.cyberfilmschool.com
American-based website which goes into some depth and detail about the processes and stages involved in making a film. Also features news and reviews on new film-making technology as well as links to related sites.

www.filmmaking.net
Another American-based website that acts as a forum for film makers, a trading post, a resource for information about techniques and tips, and a general database of knowledge about film making.

www.reelexchange.co.uk
This British website has lots of useful information and links for the prospective film maker, from finding people to assist you in making your film, script advice, help with screening your film to cameras and other equipment for sale.

Don't just stop with this information. Think of other places that may be able to help with funding and advice. Look in the *Yellow Pages*, on the Internet, in the local library. Maybe your local council has an arts and culture department or maybe there's a local arts organization down the road that can help you.

Disclaimer

The publisher has used its best endeavours to ensure that the URLs for external websites referred to in this book are correct and active at the time of going to press. However, the publisher has no responsibility for the websites and can make no guarantee that the site will remain live or that the content is, or will remain, appropriate.

Further reading

Steven Ascher (1999) *The Filmmaker's Handbook: A Comprehensive Guide for the Digital Age*, Plume Books

Raymond G. Frensham (2003) *Teach Yourself Screenwriting*, Hodder & Stoughton Educational

Barry Hampe (1997) *Making Documentary Film and Reality Videos: A Practical Guide to Planning, Filming, and Editing Documentaries of Real Events*, Owl Paperbacks

Declan McGrath (2001) *Editing and Post Production*, Focal Press

Greg Merritt (1998) *Film Production: The Complete Uncensored Guide to Filmmaking*, Lone Eagle Publishing Company

Gerald Millerson (1994) *Video Camera Techniques*, Focal Press

Robert B. Musburger (1998) *Single-camera Video Production*, Focal Press

index